"After centuries of women's work being written out of history, *The Women Who Made New York* gracefully and passionately rewrites that wrong. For anyone who loves this city or any city at all, this book is both a public service and a pleasure."

—IRIN CARMON, *New York Times* bestselling co-author of *The Notorious RBG: The Life and Times of Ruth Bader Ginsburg*

"What an inventive and important book! And long overdue. Ms. Scelfo has produced a history of New York City which we've never read, filled with insightful portraits of the women who influenced all facets of our city. Page after page is filled with a thrilling sense of discovery, as you realize the extent of contributors who have remained unheralded. This book is the definition of a must-read!"

—NANCY BASS WYDEN, co-owner of the Strand Bookstore, New York City

"A welcome antidote to male-centered history, *The Women Who Made New York* should be taught in every New York high school. I long for the day when books like this become unnecessary."

—DAVID BYRNE, award-winning composer, songwriter, singer, and author, best known for being the frontman of the Talking Heads

"These women were the original prizefighters—the trailblazers and visionaries who built the best city in the world. If you want to keep believing that New York was made by only men . . . well, don't read this book."

—JESSICA BENNETT, *New York Times* columnist and author of *Feminist Fight Club*

"Finally finally finally: the mighty women whose formidable ghosts still walk the streets of New York get their due. A rollicking and necessary book."

—VIRGINIA HEFFERNAN, *New York Times Magazine* contributor and author of *Magic and Loss: The Internet as Art*

"How can we begin to contemplate New York's history without including the women who helped build it? Julie Scelfo makes clear that without the contributions of some famous and not-so-famous women, the city would not exist as we know it. Taken together, these brief biographies reveal a dynamism and diversity as rich as New York City itself."

—VALERIE PALEY, Chief Historian and Director of the Center for Women's History at the New-York Historical Society

THE WOMEN WHO MADE NEW YORK

JULIE SCELFO | ART BY HALLIE HEALD

SEAL PRESS

ISBN 978-1-58005-653-3

Library of Congress Cataloging-in-Publication Data is available.

Published by
SEAL PRESS
An Imprint of Perseus Books
A Hachette Book Group Company
1700 Fourth Street
Berkeley, California
Sealpress.com

Cover Design: Jeff Miller, Faceout Studio
Interior Design: Emily Weigel, Faceout Studio
Interior Production: Domini Dragoone and Tabitha Lahr

Printed in China by RR Donnelley
Distributed by Publishers Group West

For Alice, my grandmother, whom I never got to know, and for all the other women without whom my New York—and yours—wouldn't be

And for my Brooklyn boys

CONTENTS

INTRODUCTION

Read any history of New York City and you will read about men. You will read about male political leaders and male activists and male cultural tastemakers, all lauded for creating the most exciting and influential city in the world.

The contributions of men are important, yes. But try for a moment to envision the City without all the women who, over four centuries, wielded pencils and rulers, hammers and washboards, frying pans and guitars. Would NYC look and sound and feel the same? Well, no, actually. Would it have any art museums or dance companies? Would clothing still be so precious that most people would own only one outfit? Would the Brooklyn Bridge be the greatest engineering project never completed? How would the skyline look? Would there be takeout? And who would have stemmed the tide of disease and rescued abandoned children, never mind paraded topless across the bar at Billy's?

In short, New York City would not be what it is without the group Simone de Beauvoir only hypothetically dubbed the "second sex." And even if men had found a way to magically reproduce without their estrogen-besotted associates, the City would be something altogether different, like a plate of rice and beans without the beans. Leaving women out of the story gives a false impression of how NYC was built. This volume aims to fix that.

This is the story of the women who made New York City the cultural epicenter of the world—both literally and metaphorically. Many are famous, like Billie Holiday and Eleanor Roosevelt. Others led quieter, private lives, but were just as influential—like Emily Warren Roebling, who completed the construction of the Brooklyn Bridge after her engineer husband became ill.

When Seal Press asked me to create a list of the twenty-five women who most contributed to the creation of our extraordinary Gotham, my initial thought was: "Easy!" I immediately thought of Ruth Bader Ginsburg, Nan Goldin, Judith Jamison, Eliza Jumel, Yuri Kochiyama, Margaret Mead, Bernadette Peters, Letty Cottin Pogrebin, Sonia Sotomayor, Harriet Tubman, Lauren Bacall, Ellen V. Futter, and Sylvia Woods.

But as I dove into my research, I turned up more and more women I'd never even heard of and yet without whom New York City would not be what it is today. Such as Hetty Green, the so-called "Witch of Wall Street," who helped save the banks in 1907. And Anne Northup, wife of *Twelve Years a Slave* author Solomon Northup and a professional cook, who brought sophisticated cuisine to New Yorkers' palates. And Agnes Chan, the City's first female Asian American police officer. And Mary Schmidt Campbell, who revitalized 125th Street and Tisch School of the Arts, New York University's important film school.

The more I searched, the more I realized that there have been hundreds, thousands—tens of thousands of women who have contributed to the making of the Big Apple in so many different, important ways. But how to choose whom to feature? How to present all their gifts?

It would take years to create a comprehensive research volume. So, to narrow the mass of material down to a concise, easily digestible (and, hopefully, fun-to-read) list, I had to develop very specific criteria for who would, and would not, be included.

I opted against identifying "firsts"; rather, I selected women without whom an important part of New York would not exist, or at least not be the same. While someone like Chan broke an important barrier and undoubtedly deserves our gratitude, the NYPD was up and running long before she got there.

Lauren Bacall was surely an iconic actress and celebrated City personality, but did her legacy particularly shape New York? And, yes, two Supreme Court justices with enormous influence grew up in NYC, but isn't their influence more on the nation as a whole as opposed to specifically on the City? Ditto Harriet Tubman. So, with a bit of anguish, I crossed these remarkable women off my list.

Casting my net as far and wide as possible, I talked to people who studied specific aspects of the City's history (like musical theater, law enforcement, and education), social justice movements (like immigration, labor, abolitionism, suffrage, and LGBTQ concerns), groups that represented various professions (including the New York City Bar Association and the NYPD Policewomen's Endowment Association), and organizations devoted to individual ethnic groups (like the Museum of Chinese in America [MOCA], the Studio Museum in Harlem, El Museo del Barrio, the National Museum of the American Indian, and the Schomburg Center for Research in Black Culture).

I also consulted architects and city planners and zoning specialists who believe, rightfully so, that the credit for building New York should go primarily to those who designed buildings, parks, and memorials *and* those who crafted the legislation, zoning policies, and budgets that made it possible for the physical city to be brought to life. These underrecognized hero(in)es include women like Sylvia Deutsch, MaryAnne Gilmartin, Janette Sadik-Khan, Billie Tsien, and, most recently, Annabelle Selldorf. (As for the latter, her handsome recycling facility in Brooklyn reshaped the City's expectation for municipal projects in the twenty-first century.)

To be sure, those women deserve credit for creating the physical body of New York. (Note that the Beverly Willis Architecture Foundation established their own informative list of significant projects designed by women.) But, to my mind, the essence of New York City resides in its soul. What would NYC be without it?

To me, part of that soul derives from the fact that the City has long been a place of transformation. For centuries New York has been the place where immigrants come in search of a better life. It's also where individuals have been able to finally find themselves—or undertake complete reinvention.

While an endless number of writers, from Walt Whitman to Ada Calhoun, have tried to describe the miracle that is New York, I think Colson Whitehead singled out something essential when he wrote, two months after the World Trade Center attack: "There are eight million naked cities in this naked city." He observed how "you start building your private New York the first time you lay eyes on it." The coffee shop where you waited for a job interview. The drugstore where you buy gum and imported magazines. "Thousands of people pass that storefront every day, each one haunting the streets of his or her own New York, not one of them seeing the same thing."

For every last straggler, New York has offered a unique blend of promise and despair, screaming skyscrapers and gritty sidewalks, Turkish coffee and Sichuan shrimp. The New York that exists in my mind and heart is the place where, during my first visit from Virginia at the age of twelve, I witnessed taxi drivers fighting in several languages, marveled at professional ballerinas in the Capezio store trying on pointe shoes, and, as I inhaled the funky smells and absorbed the cacophony, felt, for the first time, completely at home.

My New York was on Bleecker Street, where artists in slashed t-shirts peddled trash-sculptures; it was inside the Craft Caravan, where I bought African tribal jewelry; and it was the Spanish restaurant in SoHo where my groovy aunt shared our teeming plate of mussels with customers at the next table, infuriating the surly, chain-smoking waitress.

It was in the awestruck feeling a few years later of walking across Columbia University's stately campus, my belongings in a black garbage bag over my shoulder, and in the hours and hours I spent in the Barnard library and the Strand Bookstore waking up to the world around me.

My New York is in the bars on Columbus Avenue, where I drank myself into oblivion before stumbling home arm-in-arm with my best friend, delighted by the sparkling sidewalks and availability of a hot slice from Koronet at 2:00 AM. My New York was inside the Limelight nightclub, being momentarily blocked from the exit by a guy with a foot-long spike through his head; in the wondrous displays at Balducci's, the long-gone Italian food emporium on Sixth Avenue at 9th Street where even the stock boys were experts on exotic vegetables; awaiting the inevitable stomach flip during a weekly elevator ride to a job on the forty-fifth floor of the former Pan Am Building; getting high on the hazy, marijuana smoke–filled dance floor at Marylou's; and, memorably, standing on the middle of the Brooklyn Bridge where, while sharing a slice of birthday cake on a freezing November night with the man who was to become my husband, seeing a pack of young men jauntily trot past, clad only in their boxers.

My New York wasn't always pretty or kind. CBGB's may have been hip, but during a brutal summer heat wave, a few hours spent in its airless space waiting to see the noise-metal trio Unsane brought on heatstroke. A wrong turn down to the cellar of a Pakistani restaurant in Midwood, Brooklyn, led me to a destitute family, living on the dirt floor. And then there was the drunkard on the downtown sidewalk who, pants around his ankles and brandishing his personal weapon, refused to let me pass. Or another skell who, stoned out of his mind, unzipped his pants and used the full length of the banister along a Christopher Street subway station entrance as an, ahem, scratching post.

Late one night outside a long-gone nightclub on 13th Street, there was the panic of being swept up in a crowd of male rap fans fleeing up the middle of

Fourth Avenue after a thug pumped six bullets into a man's head. And then being in a taxi stopped at a red light near the Gowanus Houses in Brooklyn, surrounded by a gang of kids, watching, stupefied, as one thrust a gun through the driver's open window and pulled the trigger—a cap gun, it turned out.

Or, on the morning of September 11, taking cover from the tsunami of gray matter after the South Tower collapsed, my surprise when a trembling priest who found the same shelter gently asked me for a cigarette.

As, over time, I became a co-owner and caretaker of the City, I began to learn how to stop taking other people's shit. Like when I exited a store on Broadway and saw a man with a pair of bolt cutters preparing to cut the steel chain securing my bike to a lamppost. "Hey, that's my bike!" I screamed as I ran toward him, drawing attention from the crowd of passersby. "Uh, sorry," he stammered, looking panicked as he tried to stash the large tool into his backpack. I continued to shame him as he hurried away, demanding: "What, did you think it was *your* bike?" A decade later, I spied a tall, skinny graffiti artist drawing on the side of my neighbor's house: he took off and I gave chase, but he quickly left me in the dust.

My New York also includes unexpected friendships with teachers and writers. Neil Postman, the acclaimed media critic, became a friend and mentor and, while I worked as his assistant, treated me to a year of lunches at Poppolini's near NYU. It includes endless sightings of the glamorous and gifted: like the time in Central Park my eye caught the sheen of silky waist-length hair before I realized it was Catherine Zeta-Jones, husband and family in tow; or turning around to glare at the customer who ran over my heel with her cart at Fairway and seeing an apologetic Bernadette Peters; or when, while touring a townhouse for sale in Park Slope, the realtor introduced me to the home-owner, Gloria Naylor, a writer whose work had torn open a chamber in my heart and filled it with love.

My New York includes adventures in dining, like subsisting on bargain-priced taramasalata from East Village Cheese; the first time I discovered a chaat bar at an Indian gala; getting to go inside Floyd Cardoz's spice room at Tabla restaurant with Dorothy Kalins, the founding editor of *Saveur* magazine; and being whirled around the ballroom floor after dinner at the Waldorf Astoria hotel.

My New York includes romantic moments, like the time, returning from a temp paralegal job in Midtown and dressed in a navy silk dress, I found myself trapped in a subway station by torrential rain—until a grandfatherly stranger with an umbrella offered to walk me home. He put his arm around my waist, led me three blocks through the downpour, and, with a mischievous smile, swept me up the stoop to my sublet door. Charmed by his apparent delight, I paused before stepping inside to bestow a quick kiss on his cheek.

My New York is home to the hard-core: not necessarily the punks with safety pins in their noses tromping down St. Mark's in their Doc Martens, but the sandhogs who descend sixty stories underground to blast tunnels in the dark, or the lab workers at the NYC Medical Examiner's office who, after 9/11, looked death straight in eye, day after day after day, analyzing more lab samples than previously seen in the department's entire history. Hard-core are the cops in my neighborhood precinct who, among residents fleeing gunshots at a local park, instantly turned and ran *toward* the gunfire. It's Marlith Rios, a single mother from Peru who spent decades vacuuming office buildings at night so she could feed her sons and make a safe home for them in Queens. It's Dr. Jennifer Mathur, a forensic psychologist at the psychiatric emergency room at Bellevue Hospital, who daily treats society's most deranged individuals, sometimes immediately after they complete grisly crimes. It's Eileen Myles, in her sixty-sixth year, reading her poems at St. Mark's Church. It's Marlon James changing his clothes in a bookstore bathroom, persevering through alienation and multiple rejections of his first novel only to eventually win numerous top literary honors.

That is really the best part of New York: how it's filled with magic. Finding chalk sidewalk messages from De La Vega outside your apartment. A dead Christmas tree, deposited in a trash can, joyfully presiding over a snowy street corner. Bumping into Al Franken at the airport, who offers a ride home. The bulk foods guy at Sahadi's Fine Foods handing my stroller-parked toddler his own bag of olives. Resonant chamber music from a neighbor's cello wafting out an open window. And watching the other tortured, twentysomething misfits grow up to win Pulitzers, run companies, and write Broadway shows. Every day, a new concert, someone giving a reading, an opening to attend; and every week, news of yet another old haunt closing down.

So much of the City has changed: Union Square, the site of historic labor protests, is now home to a Babies"R"Us and Barnes & Noble. Bleecker Street, home of Rebel Rebel Records, is now a high-end mall. But scrappy creatives can still be found running pop-up shops in NoLIta (North of Little Italy) and building new communities in Bushwick, Brooklyn. Taxicabs are still driven by hopeful immigrants, some more recently arrived than others. And in the West Village, you can still observe intoxicated lovers pausing in a doorway to taste one another's mouths.

I am the descendant of many who came through New York. Among them: a Sicilian couple who lived with their five children in a tenement on Hester Street; a couple from Napoli whose son married an Irish-German girl from East New York; a Kabbalah-studying Jew from the Ukraine who practiced Sant Mat and followed the Maharishi Mahesh Yogi; and a Russian boy who, after the Bolshevik Revolution, sailed alone at sixteen to Ellis Island, before eventually finding work as a painter in Westchester County. His daughter Alice was born in 1930, got married at sixteen; a mother of two by nineteen, she wanted something more. Despite the sexism of the "Mad Men" era, she managed to build a career in education publishing, and was one of the first female members of the Book Industry Guild. One day in the early 1970s she arrived at a meeting only to find a sign declaring the space MEN-ONLY. Having earned her colleaugues' respect, or perhaps their desire, or, most likely, some messy combination of both—the group of several dozen men promptly stood up and abandoned quarters, seeking another place to meet.

Slowly, very slowly, those men, and many more like them, are overcoming centuries of tradition (and, let's face it, some lingering cave-era biology) and making space for women like Alice, my grandmother. Making space for all women, like those in this book. Without their contributions—as well as the contributions of countless others, including those who were deprived of recognition and whose names are lost to history—the New York City we know and love would be an entirely different place.

This book is merely a first step, a history that is unavoidably incomplete. In order to continue this her-story, I invite you to visit www.webuiltnewyork.com, where, with your help, we can continue recognizing the contributions of all our grandmothers, mothers, and sisters.

JULIE SCELFO

New York City, 2016

THE SETTLER

In 1639, frustrated by the oppressive religious climate in her native England, LADY DEBORAH MOODY (1583–1659), a widow in her fifties and the daughter of a wealthy, well-connected family, sailed with her grown son to the New England colonies. A member of the then-radical sect of Protestantism known as Anabaptism (which held that only adult believers—and not children— should accept baptism), she settled in Massachusetts among the Puritans, where she soon found their practice of religious persecution equally intolerable.

Moody, a single woman, was called out—and exiled—for refusing to accept the dominant church's belief in baptizing children, so she organized a group of like-minded adherents to move far away to the Dutch colony of New Netherland.

In 1643, after an arduous journey of about 230 miles, Moody and her followers set up camp on the eastern reaches of what we now know as Brooklyn. But after being soon attacked by Native American Indians, they sought refuge even further west in New Amersfoort, an independent Dutch colony that in later years became the neighborhood known as Flatlands.

In 1645, Moody, who had by then earned the confidence of New Amersfoort governor Willem Kieft, became the first woman in the New World to receive a land grant to start her own settlement, located farther south in the then-unoccupied southern region of the borough, all the way to the Atlantic shore. That same year she officially established the town of Gravesend, writing the town charter, planning a design for the roads and lots, and starting a school and a town hall government. The town was substantial in size, and may have included what are now known as the neighborhoods of Bensonhurst, Sheepshead Bay, Midwood, and Coney Island.

Moody's achievement was remarkable for several reasons. First, her town charter was in English, not Dutch, which indicated a willingness on the part of the Dutch leaders to coexist with a British neighbor. Second, the town patent granted by Kieft permitted complete religious freedom; a novelty in an age of religious fervor, this freedom was tested on several occasions when Moody provided refuge for visiting Quaker missionaries. And third, the physical layout she implemented—based on Kent, England, with a town square and twenty-eight equal parcels of land—made it one of the first towns in the New World with a square block plan, a model so useful it was later repeated in numerous other cities.

While the area settled by Moody remained largely rural for more than two hundred years, by 1894 it was one of the six towns consolidated into the city of Brooklyn, which was incorporated into New York City four years later. And though Gravesend today boasts a large Sephardic Jewish population, multimillion-dollar homes, Italian specialty food stores, and the world famous Coney Island Boardwalk, the town of Gravesend still retains the heart of the layout Moody established in the seventeenth century.

YOU, SIR! HOW DARE YOU ENTER MY HOUSE IN MY TOWN AND TELL ME HOW TO RUN MY CHURCH! IF I WISH TO GIVE COMFORT AND A PLACE TO WORSHIP, THAT IS MY BUSINESS.

—LADY DEBORAH MOODY, CIRCA 1650

THE REVOLUTIONARY

MARGARET CORBIN (1751–1800) and her brother were raised by an uncle after a violent Native American raid on her family's Pennsylvania homestead left them orphaned—her father killed and her mother captured—when she was only four or five. Years later, it was perhaps fear of losing another loved one that led Margaret to follow her husband, John Corbin, to New York to join the fight underway for independence from Great Britain.

On November 16, 1776, at Fort Washington, near the northern tip of Manhattan Island, twenty-five-year-old Corbin stood with John at his cannon when approximately 2,900 Continental troops, led by General George Washington, tried to defend New York from an onslaught by roughly eight thousand British and Hessian soldiers.

The Battle of Fort Washington was fierce. Corbin helped her husband repeatedly clean and load the massive weapon before he fired. As Hessian troops ascended the ridge, overpowering the Continentals with force, John was fatally shot, crumpling to the ground. But instead of collapsing with grief, Corbin continued to arm and fire the gunnery, displaying what a later report would describe as "fortitude and virtue enough to supply the place of her husband." The battle was said to have lasted more than two and a half hours.

Despite being vastly outnumbered, Corbin and the other Continentals continued to hold off their foes—during which time her husband's body still lay dead at her feet. She was eventually hit by grapeshot, a cluster of small cannon balls, which tore through her left breast and shoulder, nearly severing her arm.

When the Continentals ultimately surrendered Manhattan, Corbin and fellow surviving soldiers were captured and taken prisoner. At some point she was paroled and received medical treatment in Philadelphia. She remained crippled for the rest of her life, having lost the use of her arm.

In 1779, Congress determined that Corbin, who was unable to bathe or dress herself, deserved a regular pension, and granted her "one half of the monthly pay drawn by a soldier in the service of these States, and that she receive out of the public stores one complete suit of cloaths [sic] or the value thereof in money."

She was also assigned to the Corps of Invalids, a regiment of soldiers unable to perform battlefield duties but who could work as guards and provide training to new soldiers. "Captain Molly," as she came to be known, was assigned to West Point; she lived nearby until her death in 1800.

Corbin received recognition from her military contemporaries—as evidenced by both correspondence between military officials and their eventual awarding her a full monthly ration of rum and whiskey, despite the half ration of pay. And yet, sadly, she died poor and in obscurity, likely owing to what locals described as heavy drinking, infrequent bathing, and a cantankerous personality.

As the result of efforts by the Daughters of the American Revolution, Corbin's remains were discovered and identified by the wounds she had sustained in battle. She was then reburied with full military honors at the cemetery of the U.S. Military Academy at West Point. A bronze plaque commemorating her courage—and her status as the first woman to fight as a solider in the Revolutionary War— was installed near the battle site in what is now Fort Tryon Park.

THE CARETAKERS

DR. ELIZABETH BLACKWELL (1821–1910), the first female MD in the United States, hung out her shingle on University Place in 1851. Unfortunately, she did not attract patients, and so endured abject poverty and disapproving remarks from passersby—all while Madame Restell (a.k.a. Ann Trow), an abortionist with no medical training, accumulated a vast fortune from her practice. Finally, Blackwell managed to open a free dispensary serving the impoverished slum-dwellers of the Eleventh Ward, a teeming neighborhood of squalid tenements on Manhattan's Lower East Side. The one-room dispensary, near what is now Tompkins Square, was immediately inundated by scores of mostly Irish and German immigrants suffering from cholera, tuberculosis, and typhoid. In addition to seeing patients and making deathbed house calls, Blackwell also began sending nurses into slums to teach residents about personal hygiene.

After several years of hustling and fund-raising—she was said to possess such a sterling character that many leading male physicians and philanthropists agreed to back her—in 1857 Blackwell established a full-fledged hospital: the New York Infirmary for Indigent Women and Children, which would eventually serve more than one million patients over its 139 years. After a number of mergers and acquisitions over the years, it still exists as part of New York-Presbyterian/Lower Manhattan Hospital.

Within the hospital, Blackwell also established a training facility for female doctors; in 1868, it expanded into a medical college for women—the first four-year medical program in the nation, as it happens. Some of her graduates would go on to make even greater strides in public health. One of them, in fact, would become one of the most important innovators in medical history: Sara Josephine Baker.

At the turn of the century, the medical profession was devoted mainly to treating sickness; preventing people from getting sick in the first place wasn't physicians' primary focus. **DR. SARA JOSEPHINE BAKER** (1873–1945), who joined the City's health department in 1901, was among the first to fully appreciate the strong connection between hygiene and the spread of disease. And so, she devised public health programs that made heavily populated neighborhoods more sanitary and, indeed, livable.

Early on, Baker was charged with ensuring residents of the Lower East Side got smallpox vaccines, but transients on the Bowery refused the shots. So Baker, an intrepid problem-solver, led a team on rounds at flophouses long after midnight— so they could inoculate the men before they were awake enough to protest.

DR. SARA JOSEPHINE BAKER

I AM GLAD I, AND NOT ANOTHER, HAVE TO BEAR THIS PIONEER WORK. I UNDERSTAND NOW WHY THIS LIFE HAS NEVER BEEN LIVED BEFORE. IT *IS* HARD, WITH NO SUPPORT BUT A HIGH PURPOSE, TO LOVE AGAINST EVERY SPECIES OF SOCIAL OPPOSITION.

—ELIZABETH BLACKWELL, 1853

In 1907 Baker was tasked with apprehending Mary Mallon, a typhoid-carrying cook known as Typhoid Mary, who refused to believe she carried something called a "germ," and so continued preparing food around the City. Baker chased her through the streets until she caught her; once the patient was installed in the back of an ambulance, Baker sat on top of her all the way to the hospital to ensure she didn't escape.

Soon after, the health department became concerned with the City's extraordinary infant death rate. Wanting to test her prevention hypothesis, Baker sent thirty nurses into a "complicated, filthy, sunless, and stifling nest of tenements on the Lower East Side" to teach immigrant mothers about hygiene, ventilation, safety measures (like not putting babies to sleep in long Victorian gowns in which they overheated and sometimes strangled themselves while sleeping), and breast-feeding; by the end of the summer, the area had reported 1,200 fewer infant deaths than the previous year. As a result, the City created a Bureau of Child Hygiene, installing Baker as its head; during her tenure there she solved so many problems the bureau became a model replicated by other states and the federal government.

By the time Baker retired in 1923, New York City had the lowest infant mortality rate of any major American city, making it a place where people could survive and thrive—despite the crowded conditions.

A doctor wasn't always required to address the plights of early city-dwellers.

In 1806, two years after Alexander Hamilton, a founding father, was famously killed by Aaron Burr in a duel, **ELIZABETH HAMILTON** (1757–1854), Alexander's widow and a member of the state's prominent Schuyler family, joined with two of her friends to cofound an organization devoted to caring for some of the hundreds of orphans then roaming New York City streets.

Through the Orphan Asylum Society (OAS), Hamilton, together with Isabella Graham and Johanna Bethune, rented a two-story frame house on what is now known as Barrow Street, hired a married couple to live there, and took in sixteen children who, like Hamilton's husband, had been orphaned at a young age.

OAS was among the first institutions to implement caregiving in what's known as the "cottage system," a method that roughly approximates family life in a home setting instead of forcing individuals to live warehoused in an institution—a change that would have lasting consequences for a wide variety of New Yorkers who require extra support.

It took about three more decades before other progressive city-dwellers mobilized to assist a more diverse array of needy children. In 1835, the Society for the Relief of Half-Orphan and Destitute Children was established to support poor kids of single parents. In 1836, Quaker women opened New York's Colored Orphan Asylum Society, the first orphanage in the City for black children—who, according to historian William Seraile, may have been parentless in even greater numbers than were white children.

Six decades later, in 1889, **MOTHER CABRINI** (1850–1917), the Catholic sister who would later become a saint—Saint Frances Xavier Cabrini—arrived in New York with several of her missionary sisters to assist struggling and impoverished Italian immigrants, who, viewed as nonwhites, faced relentless discrimination. But their intentions encountered immediate pushback: although Pope Leo XIII had sent Cabrini to work in New York, once they arrived the local archbishop told her fellow Missionary Sisters of the Sacred Heart of Jesus, which Cabrini had founded in 1880, to return to Italy. With no helpmates, money, or institutional support, Mother Cabrini traversed the streets of Manhattan on her own, begging for alms. Before long she also organized catechism classes at St. Joachim's Church in Little Italy and provided necessities to orphan children. Within a few years, she opened an Italian orphanage, a tiny hospital, and a free school.

Her peaceful demeanor was such that acolytes claimed everything she did had the quality of a prayer. And yet, she also demonstrated savvy entrepreneurial skills, despite suffering ill health for most of her life. She established a residence for orphaned children on East 59th Street. In 1899, she opened a boarding school for girls (which eventually became Mother Cabrini High School) in Washington Heights, an area now home to many immigrants from the Dominican Republic. She died in 1917 at the age of sixty-seven.

Mother Cabrini's accomplishments and legacy weren't limited to her work in New York; her impact extended across the country, as well as to Central and South America. In 1946 she was canonized as Saint Frances Xavier Cabrini; in 1950, the Vatican declared her patroness of immigrants. Today, 130-plus years later, the nuns of the Cabrini order remain at the forefront of the Catholic social justice movement in fifteen countries on six continents, while thousands of Catholic pilgrims visit the St. Frances X. Cabrini Shrine in Upper Manhattan, which contains a recently restored glass tile mosaic, as well as her corpus (with a wax head) displayed in a glass coffin.

⁂

In 1932 **CLARA HALE** (1905–1992), twenty-seven and newly widowed, wanted to give her children the same nurturing and support she and her four siblings had received from her own widowed mother in Philadelphia, but the handful of cleaning jobs she relied on for financial support greatly limited that possibility. So she quit those jobs and opened a day care in her Harlem home.

Given the high poverty rates among her neighbors, and how many of them were forced to travel long distances for work, Hale had no shortage of customers. But Clara's day care was more than just a safe place, and Hale had a generous spirit and a gift for understanding children's needs. She offered such a nurturing environment that many of her charges—whose parents, often single mothers themselves, were perpetually exhausted—remained with her for the entire work week, returning to their own mothers only on the weekends.

In the 1940s, Hale began fostering a number of children in her Harlem community. She also taught parenting classes and helped find permanent, quality placements for homeless children. She continued this work throughout the 1950s, eventually taking in and lovingly raising more than forty foster kids.

In 1969 Hale's biological daughter, Lorraine, brought home a drug-addicted mother and child; Hale nursed them back to wellness. As word of this care spread, more babies born with drug addictions were sent to Hale for similar aid, and a year later, in 1970, she founded Hale House, a fully licensed child-care facility. A few years after that she purchased a five-story home and opened her doors, free of charge, to any addicted child. She cared for these children until they were healthy, at which point she tried to reunite them with family members, or, if that wasn't possible, helped them find families interested in adoption. Many of these children have since reflected on how assiduously "Mother Hale," as she was known, ensured every adoptive family was the right match for each child; she wasn't above turning away families she considered not good enough for "her" babies.

Beginning in the 1980s, she expanded her care to include infants who'd lost their parents to HIV/AIDS—or who themselves were born with HIV. She later also provided assistance to troubled teens, and started a variety of programs to help keep women on track after detoxification. In all her years of work, Hale helped over one thousand young citizens of New York, her Hale House serving as a beacon to countless families during some of the City's darkest periods.

THE BUILDERS

In 1869, construction began on John A. Roebling's design of the Brooklyn Bridge. That same year, Roebling died as a result of an injury sustained on-site, at which point his son, Washington Roebling, assumed the role of chief engineer. When Washington fell ill three years later, in 1872, several politicians called for his ouster—the project, considered the greatest construction and engineering feat of the nineteenth century, had already seen exorbitant cost overruns and the deaths of numerous workers. But all the builders knew a change in command would have inevitably created further delays and even more complications.

Enter **EMILY WARREN ROEBLING** (1843–1903), Washington's wife, a graduate of the prestigious Georgetown Visitation Convent—today called the Georgetown Visitation Preparatory School—and, according to her husband, "a woman of infinite tact and wisest counsel." Initially, she served as Washington's secretary, taking dictation and making site visits so as to deliver his notes and gather updates. But in short order Emily became so well versed in subjects like catenary curves, stress analysis, and cable construction that she began solving all manner of site problems on her own—eventually earning the respect of the many bigwigs associated with the project, and, many believe, actually embodying the role of chief engineer, even though her husband retained the title.

Upon the bridge's opening in 1883, Emily received the honor of being the first person to cross it; later, a plaque honoring all three members of the Roebling family was installed on the east-side tower of the bridge, where it remains today. It reads: "Back of every great work we can find the self-sacrificing devotion of a woman."

In 1893, **LILLIAN WALD** (1867–1940), a native of Ohio intent on becoming a doctor, was led by a child to attend to a gravely ill woman in a dilapidated tenement on the Lower East Side. The needs in the neighborhood were so great that she jettisoned her career plans and immediately moved to the impoverished area. Two years later, with her nursing friend Mary Brewster, Wald opened what became the legendary Henry Street Settlement, a neighborhood center on the Lower East Side where educated women lived and worked among the poor; it was also the first organization in the United States to staff nurses who treated at home those too poor or ill to visit a doctor.

Wald learned a great deal from her time living among the poor. Ever insightful, she recognized that children's difficulties in school didn't result from a flaw in character but were a byproduct of their impoverished, wretched living conditions. (At one point, the Lower East Side had the highest population density in the world and was said to be more crowded than the slums of

EMILY WARREN ROEBLING

Calcutta.) So she undertook a series of measures to provide them with better health and well-being. To prevent sick children from spreading disease, she first installed a nurse in one public school—then successfully lobbied the City to follow suit in all others. Recognizing how hunger causes an array of emotional and behavioral problems that interfere with learning, she convinced the City to provide school lunches. When a boy complained that he couldn't do his homework because his sister was always using the family's one table, she allocated rooms at Henry Street for study halls and pressed the Board of Education to provide study halls in schools. She also devised and brought about public playgrounds, special classes for children with extra needs, and summer camps in the country.

Wald's concern about the welfare of poor New Yorkers stemmed as much from her belief in democracy as it did from altruism. "As a nation," she said, "we must rise or fall as we serve or fail these future citizens."

In short, Wald invented the idea of growing human capital as an essential civic task, in turn paving the way for the field of social work. In her fight against child labor, she proposed—to her friend President Roosevelt—a federal children's bureau to protect child welfare, which was realized in the subsequent administration. The nonprofit home health care service she created at Henry Street in time became the Visiting Nurse Service, which over the decades played a central role in containing city outbreaks of polio, influenza, and AIDS.

AS A NATION, WE MUST RISE OR FALL AS WE SERVE OR FAIL THESE FUTURE CITIZENS.

—LILLIAN WALD, 1915

It wasn't just individuals who benefited from disease no longer being the dire threat it had always been; the City itself benefitted from having a more reliable workforce. With that workforce in place, which was essential to the second industrial revolution, the City burgeoned into a base for numerous industries, like finance and fashion. Ultimately, as nurse and creative visionary, Lillian invented an array of practices, including the career of public health nurse, that enabled the City to become a flourishing, functioning metropolis.

Every visitor to NYC—even those who just fly over it—have seen the handiwork of commercial real estate broker **MARY ANN TIGHE** (b. 1948) (pronounced "tie").

An Italian American raised in the South Bronx, Tighe is the CEO of the New York Tri-State Region of CBRE, the world's largest commercial real estate services firm; she has also been repeatedly named, by *Crain's New York Business*, one of the City's most powerful women.

In her thirty-one-plus years in the real estate industry, Tighe has been responsible for ninety-three million square feet of commercial real estate transactions. One example of her impact: Christie's auction house is headquartered in Rockefeller Center, the site of an old garage, because Tighe envisioned its possibility—and then convinced numerous people to spend hundreds of millions of dollars to make it happen.

Tighe has also orchestrated several projects that transformed the City's skyline, including the move by chic publishing behemoth Condé Nast to 4 Times Square during the mid-nineties—an era when 42nd Street was still ruled by skells and derelict peepshows. That deal was widely viewed as the cornerstone to the City's efforts to clean up and "revitalize" Times Square, a transformation that successfully ushered in the banal—but decidedly cleaner and safer—Disneyfication of the neighborhood.

In a more recent occurrence: with the City still in mourning after the September 11 attack, the financial fate of Lower Manhattan was in jeopardy given how downtown had become so deeply associated with sadness. And so, Tighe convinced Condé Nast to relocate again, this time to 1 World Trade Center, a move that boosted the City's efforts to redevelop the site. So far, she remains the only woman to serve as chair of the Real Estate Board of New York (REBNY), one of the City's most powerful and historic trade groups. "One of the great delights of New York is its embrace of a good idea," Tighe told me. "You show up with a good idea or a talent, and New York will find a use for both."

While Mary Ann Tighe brokered the doings of private developers, **AMANDA M. BURDEN** (b. 1944), the Commissioner of NYC's Department of City Planning during the Bloomberg administration, undertook the largest planning effort since 1961 and spearheaded the City's commitment to creating high-quality public open space. After her appointment in 2002, she rescued the elevated rail line that had been ordered demolished by Mayor Rudolph Giuliani and convinced thirty-three separate developers to cooperate in the opening of the High Line park. To prepare for what her department estimated would be one million more City residents by 2030, she rezoned 40 percent of all blocks and passed regulations ensuring 90 percent of all new development would be within a ten-minute walk to the subway—a remarkable feat considering a single zoning change can entail numerous studies and years of back-and-forth with city officials in other departments. To reclaim the water-front for public use and enjoyment, she wrote a plan for all 520 miles of it—the longest and most diverse waterfront in the U.S.—which converted what for decades had been lingering industrial eyesores into a vast array of public parks. She also helped New York once again compete with the world's greatest cities by encouraging the hiring of top-flight architects, like Frank Gehry, Richard Rogers, and Diller Scofidio + Renfro; pushing for ambitious architecture; and rejecting components of projects that failed to live up to her high standards.

Since Burden was born into an affluent family and is the daughter of style icon Babe Paley, the most famous of Truman Capote's coterie of "swans," she was often dismissed as nothing more than a socialite. While it is true that Burden's romantic life and attendance at glamorous parties was admiringly catalogued in *Vogue*, that scarlet S has obscured her thirty-year career in urban planning—a career launched when she won an award for her Columbia University master's thesis on the far-from-glamorous subject of solid waste. In the 1980s, she oversaw the design of the resplendent ninety-two-acre Battery Park City, which transformed lower Manhattan—formerly desolate on the weekends—into a livable, vibrant, active waterfront neighborhood.

Developers frequently decried the power she wielded, as well as her unrelenting insistence on making all projects great. But many others credit her with initiating and producing the most comprehensive, strategic planning the City has enjoyed in a century.

"People need places to mix, to engage, to meet, to feel comfortable, to experience nature, to breathe clean air and see other people," she told me. "Public open spaces make cities work."

All city residents—and not just those who can afford a Park Avenue address—deserve good design, she insists. "It's as important on Fulton Street in Bedford-Stuyvesant, Brooklyn, as it is on Melrose Avenue in the Bronx."

THE LIBERATORS

As early as the 1820s, women in New York began agitating for liberation, first from the perversity of slavery, then from patriarchy.

After spending years immersed in the worlds of abolitionists and jurists, **ELIZABETH CADY STANTON** (1815–1902), vividly aware of the many social and legal injustices perpetrated against women, was instrumental in creating what became the first women's rights convention: the Seneca Falls Convention of 1848. A few years later Stanton joined forces with **SUSAN B. ANTHONY** (1820–1906); they were an interesting team. Stanton was a religious skeptic; Anthony was a working-class Quaker with progressive ideals. Stanton had a husband and a small cadre of children, whereas Anthony, who was unmarried, was unburdened by such housekeeping. Together, they proved to be a formidable force in building support for the rights of all women, regardless of upbringing.

Over the next four and a half decades, the unlikely pair became warriors for women's emancipation, galvanizing the growing women's rights movements in New York and beyond. Stanton was a bold thinker and clever strategist; Anthony, who initially felt nervous about public speaking, provided the legs for Stanton's ideas. Spurred by what biographers Geoffrey C. Ward and Ken Burns described in *Not For Ourselves Alone: The Story of Elizabeth Cady Stanton and Susan B. Anthony* as an "almost manic" level of energy, Anthony constantly traveled, rented halls, raised funds, organized petition drives, and delivered speeches—usually written by Stanton—"wherever she could drum up a crowd."

In 1862, when her husband received a federal appointment, Stanton moved to New York City, where she and Anthony helped launch *The Revolution*, a newspaper that publicized grassroots activism nationwide and overseas. They also organized meetings, gave speeches, and, tapping into the vast political and financial resources of the City, established the National Woman's Suffrage Association in 1869, under whose auspices Victoria Woodhull spoke before a Congressional committee. (We'll meet Victoria Woodhull again in the "Wall Street" chapter.)

To say Stanton and Anthony were treated harshly by the male establishment would be a profound understatement. Anthony, who came to personify the movement, routinely faced hostile mobs and received vicious threats. Her backbreaking efforts were often thoroughly degraded—as when, in 1877, presenting the ten thousand signatures she gathered from twenty-six states on a petition calling for a vote on suffrage, the all-male Congress simply laughed at her.

Having for two decades argued for universal suffrage based on the idea that it is a fundamental *human* right, the duo felt betrayed when, after the Civil War, many former political allies (like Frederick Douglass) abandoned women's suffrage in supporting the Fifteenth Amendment, which in 1870 granted black men the right to vote. Newly cynical, Stanton ruthlessly acknowledged she would embrace any political maneuvering necessary to win universal suffrage,

WE HOLD THESE
TRUTHS TO BE
SELF-EVIDENT:
THAT ALL MEN
AND WOMEN ARE
CREATED EQUAL.

—ELIZABETH CADY STANTON, 1848

even opportunistically disparaging blacks; this stance gave rise to a series of racist remarks by which Stanton is sometimes remembered.

Although neither woman lived to see American women finally get the right to vote in 1920, three-quarters of a century after Seneca Falls, Anthony took great care to document all the work they did, an important step in an era when women's contributions often went unrecorded. In ensuring the movement's history survived, she provided yet another legacy—of self-empowerment—for future generations.

Unhappy with her quiet life as a mother of three children in Westchester County, **MARGARET SANGER** (1879–1966) and her husband moved to New York City in 1911, where she discovered the movement for workers' rights and other radical thinkers like Emma Goldman, an anarchist and early advocate of female sexual empowerment.

In Manhattan, Sanger attended meetings of the Women's Committee of the New York Socialist Party. Having been trained as a nurse, she also began giving talks on women's reproductive health, mainly about preventing and treating sexually transmitted disease—information generally unavailable to poor women who couldn't afford doctors. Her speeches were so popular she was asked to turn them into a column, which she did; called "What Every Girl Should Know," it was featured in a socialist daily newspaper.

She also joined Lillian Wald and her band of nurses, who visited impoverished workers living in squalid tenements on the Lower East Side. (For more on Wald, see "The Builders" chapter.) On such visits she repeatedly encountered poor mothers who, dreading more children and further impoverishment, undertook desperate, dangerous measures to prevent or abort pregnancies. One especially heart-rending evening proved to be pivotal for Sanger. On this night, she watched a mother die from sepsis resulting from a second self-induced abortion while her three distraught children and husband looked on and wept; in attendance as well was the doctor who had previously declined the woman's pleas for information on avoiding further pregnancies. After this ordeal, Sanger, whose own mother had died young after birthing eleven children, stayed up all night roaming the streets.

"That night," she later wrote, "I knew I could not go on merely nursing, allowing mothers to suffer and die. No matter what it might cost, I was resolved to do something to change the destiny of mothers, whose miseries were vast as the sky."

So Sanger began researching female reproduction and rudimentary forms of birth control. In 1914, she began publishing a magazine called *The Woman Rebel*—despite the federal Comstock Law, which since 1873 had made it illegal to circulate anything considered obscene or immoral (and which authorities had previously used to shut down her newspaper column). After a warrant was issued for her arrest, Sanger fled to Europe, where she learned (in Holland) about more advanced forms of contraception like the diaphragm.

Soon after her return to New York in late 1915, Sanger opened the country's first birth control clinic, in Brownsville, Brooklyn. Nine days later she was arrested; after being tried and convicted, she spent thirty days in jail—all of which generated loads of press coverage. Indeed, Sanger had chosen Brooklyn as her site for a reason. Although there were states with more enlightened attitudes toward women's health than New York, Sanger knew the City's publicity potential was unparalleled; as such it was the ideal location for raising awareness among women who might not even realize their options were being withheld.

Year after year, decade after decade, Sanger tenaciously advanced her mission. In 1921, she founded the American Birth Control League; two years later, she opened the country's first stand-alone medical offices where women could receive an array of gynecological and contraceptive services from female physicians; within two decades the organizations would merge and become Planned Parenthood.

She smuggled in diaphragms from Europe, then arranged for their manufacture in America. She funded research that led to spermicidal jellies and powders. Eventually, in the 1950s—when she was in her eighties—her dedication resulted in a revolutionary, infinitely more practical form of contraception: the pill.

Not surprisingly, throughout her life she battled the Catholic Church, which used its connections in the New York Police Department to obstruct her activities (including once having her carried off the stage at Town Hall to prevent her from delivering a speech). She also battled the Comstock Law, continually finding new and inventive ways to challenge the idea that communicating about sexual health was "obscene." She battled men, like those on a New York medical committee who argued that contraceptives were "absurd, frequently dangerous, filthy, and usually unsatisfactory," adding that they threatened "personal morality and national strength"—a sentiment later echoed by former President Theodore Roosevelt.

Unfortunately, in the twenty-first century some of Sanger's heroic work has been curtailed, as fundamentalist Christians have pushed several states to pass laws privileging the rights of unborn fetuses over the rights of their mothers. All the same, there is no question that Sanger's work helped to establish New York City as the vanguard of the movement to give women ultimate sovereignty over their own bodies.

The battle over hearts and minds has been equally epic. For as long as humans have attempted to civilize one another, they have established ideas about self and others that, while useful for shaping identity, often fomented deep wells of intolerance toward difference.

As one of the few black girls among a sea of white teenagers attending Hunter High School in Manhattan in the late 1940s, **AUDRE LORDE** (1934–1992), a daughter of West Indian parents, experienced life like an outsider, both at school and at home. Her mother and father frequently spoke of their fondness for the Caribbean, and about feeling out of place in New York.

I AM DELIBERATE AND AFRAID OF NOTHING.

—AUDRE LORDE, 1973

While attending Hunter College in the 1950s, Lorde spent time with friends in Greenwich Village, sometimes hanging out at the Waldorf Cafe, which was often frequented by Amiri Baraka, Robert Earl Jones, and James Baldwin. She also began to explore her attraction to other women. But, though she lived in an era when interracial relationships were slowly gaining acceptance among the political left, homosexuality was still taboo—leaving her feeling alone and ostracized. Desperate to survive a dark depression, Lorde began to wonder "what being safe and free could mean."

In high school she had written poetry to try to work out feelings she was unable to speak. In her young adult life, as she began to accept her identity as a lesbian and poet, she challenged herself to practice the freedoms—of owning her truths—she had internally defined. And so she began setting down on paper difficult, wrenching verses about what it meant to be a member of multiple oppressed communities, and slowly she began to share them.

Over the years, while working as a librarian and raising her kids (the product

AUDRE LORDE

48

of an eight-year marriage in the 1960s), she gave voice to the oft-ignored, difficult-to-articulate experience of otherness in a series of works she initially conceived as only for herself.

While a poet-in-residence at Tougaloo College—a historic black college in Mississippi where the campus was under siege by whites who routinely shot at or arrested students for non-crimes—Lorde realized she wanted to use poetry as a weapon against social and political forces that assailed marginalized members of society. "I realized I could take my art in the realist way and make it do what I wanted," she said, "altering feelings and lives."

Over a two-decade-plus career in New York, the woman who called herself a "black, lesbian, mother, warrior, poet" fearlessly confronted love and death, self and otherness, need and fear, shining light on important truths many people were too terrified to face. She stripped away the lies of difference, showing that "liberation is not the private province of any one particular group." She did this by asking whites to confront their treatment of blacks, by asking heterosexuals to reflect on same-sex love, and by inviting prominent white feminists (like Mary Daly) to reflect on the unconscious biases and privileges inherent in a political movement they claimed was on behalf of every woman.

The poet Sapphire once recounted to an interviewer how, at a meeting of black nationalists, where many gathered men embraced centuries-old homophobic teachings, Lorde stood up and declared, "I am a lesbian," which amounted to "not just moving the mountain, it was creating a new world."

Lorde held teaching posts at multiple universities, was named New York

State Poet Laureate, and cofounded Kitchen Table: Women of Color Press in Harlem. Throughout, her pioneering message about seeing difference as an opportunity for acceptance and love—rather than for division and hate—laid the foundation on which nearly every other liberation cause in the City was built, from Third World feminism to transgenderism to pansexuality.

In her award-winning book *The Cancer Journals*, Audre Lorde chronicled her long battle with cancer—to which she ultimately succumbed at the age of just fifty-eight. Striving for meaning in identity to the end, before her death she took a new name in an African naming ceremony: Gamba Adisa, which means "Warrior: She Who Makes Her Meaning Known."

For centuries, religious leaders have taught that same-sex attraction is more than just aberrant; it's outright immoral. In the nineteenth century, Anglo-American scientists and lawyers, set on determining whether those accused of criminal sexual behavior had "a constitutional or mental defect," turned to the language of pathology. This led in 1952 to the American Psychiatric Association (APA) codifying homosexuality as a form of mental illness in the *Diagnostic and Statistical Manual of Mental Disorders* (DSM), the official handbook used by health professionals nationwide.

It was into a society with this prevailing and deeply entrenched viewpoint that **BARBARA GITTINGS** (1932–2007) was born. While growing up in

Wilmington, Delaware, she began to perceive she was homosexual—and knew this was something she could not broach with others. She turned to libraries to try to make sense of her feelings, but she found almost no information on the subject.

Still searching while in college, Gittings pored through card catalogs. Though she found a few entries under "abnormal" and "perversion," these were unhelpful, as she knew instinctively that her orientation was neither unnatural nor a choice.

One day when she was home from college, her father caught her reading a lesbian love story—Radclyffe Hall's 1928 *The Well of Loneliness*. Rather than speak about it aloud, he wrote her a letter—though they lived under one roof—demanding that she burn it. Instead, Gittings left home, moved to Philadelphia, and from there, on the weekends, she hitchhiked to Greenwich Village, where she discovered a burgeoning lesbian scene.

Around this time, Gittings found Donald Webster Cory's trailblazing book, *The Homosexual in America: A Subjective Approach*. She agreed with Cory's thinking, that gays should organize themselves, and demand their rights be upheld just like other minority groups. Then, in San Francisco, she visited a meeting held by the Daughters of Bilitis, the first lesbian civil and political rights organization in the United States (formed in 1955 in San Francisco by Phyllis Lyon and Del Martin and others). At the behest of Lyon and Martin, she returned to the East Coast and founded the pioneering New York chapter of the group in 1958.

In 1962, Gittings became editor of its publication, *The Ladder*, which served as a lifeline to lesbians throughout the country—many of whom lived in virulently homophobic communities with no other source of support; some even wrote in to say the publication kept them alive. Nonetheless, Gittings felt the founders of the group mistakenly reinforced the notion that homosexuals' sexual orientation was problematic, so she altered the content and tone of the magazine to reflect pride and self-acceptance rather than shame.

Gittings also worked to change others' views: writing to the New York Academy of Medicine in 1964, she questioned their characterization of homosexuality as a preventable and treatable illness, and chastised the organization for making the assertion without any sound scientific evidence. Year after year, she led or joined protests, objecting to the classification of homosexuality as a mental illness, at annual meetings of the APA, which publishes the DSM. Finally, in 1972, the APA agreed to host a panel where the harm and inaccuracy of the classification would be discussed. Gittings found and arranged for a closeted gay psychiatrist to come out—although wearing a disguise—onstage, at which point he asked the APA membership to acknowledge the significant population of homosexuals among its ranks.

The next year, in 1973, homosexuality was finally removed as a disorder from the DSM, thereby freeing New Yorkers—and Americans everywhere—from the corrosive and damaging view that one's self could somehow be defective or "wrong." This victory solidified Gittings's legacy as a vital force in the fight toward fully liberating all people from the effects of prejudice, discrimination and even self-hate.

THE BEACON

A descendant of Sephardic Jews from Portugal who emigrated in the late 1700s, **EMMA LAZARUS** (1849–1887) was born in New York City to a wealthy family. Her love of poetry developed from such an early age that, according to the American Academy of Poets, by the time she was a teenager she had translated works by Victor Hugo, Alexandre Dumas, and Friedrich Schiller. She also read the modern literature of Germany, Italy, and France, as well as Greek and Latin classics.

In 1867, when she was just eighteen, she published translations of German verse along with a collection of her poems; these works attracted attention from critics and poets, including Ralph Waldo Emerson, who became a friend and mentor. Over the next two decades, Lazarus wrote more poetry and other compositions (including a novel and a verse drama) and developed a deep interest in Jewish ancestry. She also became involved in helping Russian Jewish refugees housed in temporary shelters on Wards Island, which functioned as the City's primary immigration station before Ellis Island opened in 1892. In working with these refugees—seeing their troubles up close, and learning of Russian pogroms—she became deeply concerned about the plight of Jewish people.

In 1883, a Manhattan civic group raising money to build a granite pedestal for the Statue of Liberty asked Lazarus to compose a sonnet for a fund-raising auction. In penning "The New Colossus," Lazarus was able to broaden her concern to all persecuted immigrants, envisioning America as a refuge for anyone seeking a better life:

GIVE ME YOUR TIRED, YOUR POOR,

YOUR HUDDLED MASSES YEARNING TO BREATHE FREE,

THE WRETCHED REFUSE OF YOUR TEEMING SHORE,

SEND THESE, THE HOMELESS, TEMPEST-TOST TO ME,

I LIFT MY LAMP BESIDE THE GOLDEN DOOR!

The statue, a gift from the French, was intended to commemorate the U.S.–French alliance during the American Revolution; the idea of it serving as an emblem of welcoming wasn't even discussed during its dedication ceremony in 1886. Lazarus died the following year, after battling what is thought to have been Hodgkin's lymphoma. Though thereafter her work began falling into obscurity, her friend Georgina Schuyler, an art patron and great-granddaughter of Alexander Hamilton, himself an immigrant, lobbied to have Lazarus's poem affixed to the statue's pedestal.

Almost two decades later, in 1903, Schuyler succeeded, and with her own funds commissioned the poem's inscription on a bronze plaque. From that point forward, the statue—named Mother of Exiles in Lazarus's sonnet—began its journey into the world's consciousness as a symbol of America's promise for liberty to all.

At the time of the poem's creation, the poet James Russell Lowell appreciated the profundity of Lazarus's work, writing her to say that he liked the poem "much better than I like the Statue itself" because it "gives its subject a raison d'être which it wanted before quite as much as it wants a pedestal. You have set it on a noble one, saying admirably just the right word to be said, an achievement more arduous than that of the sculptor."

THE ADVOCATES

As a teenager, Elizabeth Cochran, whose father had died when she was six years old, dreamed of becoming a teacher so she could support her widowed mother. Presumably, she wasn't the only reader of *The Pittsburgh Dispatch* who felt a jolt of indignation upon reading "What Girls Are Good For," the title of an 1885 editorial that declared women would do best by staying home and performing domestic duties—citing a working woman as nothing less than "a monstrosity." But only twenty-year-old Cochran was furious enough to craft a fiery rebuttal so well written that the managing editor of the paper offered her a job, paying five dollars a week.

Assuming the pen name **NELLIE BLY** (1864–1922) after a popular song by Stephen Foster, the young woman began reporting on a number of topics relevant to women of the day, such as life in the slums, working in Pittsburgh's factories, and the bias against women inherent in divorce proceedings.

Two years later, she left for New York City determined to land a job at Joseph Pulitzer's *New York World*; after months of rejections, she finally convinced an editor to send her undercover as a pretend patient into the notorious public asylum on what was then called Blackwell's Island (now known as Roosevelt Island) in the East River.

After convincing doctors and judges she was insane, Bly spent ten days living with the other patients, enduring cruel beatings, force-feedings, and frigid baths before the *World* secured her release. She then described the treatment of patients in excruciating detail: like watching nurses drag an old woman by her hair while calling her names, or being forced to eat rancid butter. Her story proved so embarrassing to City officials that they immediately launched an investigation and increased funds to improve treatment.

Bly's exposé was soon followed by investigations into crooked lobbyists, labor abuses, mistreatment of female prisoners, and inadequate medical care for the poor.

The peak of Bly's fame came in 1889 for a headline-grabbing race around the globe modeled after Jules Verne's classic adventure novel *Around the World in 80 Days*. But it was her forging of investigative journalism, her revealing of the otherwise-unseen abuses and indignities suffered by New York's poor and marginalized, that galvanized those in power into effecting meaningful change.

During WWI, by then a woman in her fifties, she worked overseas as the first American female war correspondent. At war's end she returned to New York, where she advocated for homeless children, seeking homes for them through a column in the *New York Evening Journal*. She died at the age of fifty-seven.

⁂

The Industrial Revolution, which transformed a more agrarian society to a more mechanized one, provided much-needed employment and invigorated the

American economy—and yet also introduced new methods of exploiting workers. Factory owners, aiming to maximize profits, pushed employees to operate machinery, attach widgets, and repeat a wide array of other assembly-line tasks at ever-more efficient speeds. Given the high volume of laborers desperate for income—many of them immigrants—some NYC employers felt free to ruthlessly disregard the physical and emotional toll on workers, and simply replaced anyone who balked. Not surprisingly, the conditions resulting from this equation were appalling.

The extent of owners' disregard for human life was on stark display in Manhattan on March 25, 1911, when the City's deadliest workplace disaster to date took place on Washington Place in Greenwich Village. A fire broke out on the eighth, ninth, and tenth floors of the Asch Building, home to the Triangle Shirtwaist Factory, from which many workers, mostly young women, were unable to escape. Why? So as to reduce the likelihood of excessive breaks and theft, a main stairwell had been locked by the factory's bosses, who themselves escaped via a different stairwell before it was consumed by fire. Indeed, the foreman with the key also fled, leaving the workers trapped in an inferno.

A crowd of bystanders on the street below watched in horror as a macabre parade of women, preferring a quick end to an excruciating one, jumped to their deaths. Many of the jumpers were engulfed in flames, and blood ran in the streets. In the end a total of 146 workers would die in the Triangle Shirtwaist Factory fire, some burned alive in the factory. The incident left City residents aghast, who for the next few weeks held vigils and protests all over the City, demanding a government response.

One such meeting took place on April 2, 1911, at the Metropolitan Opera House, where tensions broke out between working-class spectators and the wealthier attendees who seemed more concerned about improving the services of the fire department than about workers' rights. Amid the discussion, **ROSE SCHNEIDERMAN** (1882–1972), a petite woman (just four foot nine) with striking red hair, took the stage to voice her concerns—and quickly transfixed the audience with her passionate indignations.

Schneiderman had experienced firsthand the pay inequality and abuses of factory work: one of four children of Polish immigrants, she had been forced at age thirteen to leave school and find employment after her father died. At the time of this gathering, she had been involved in labor activism for nearly a decade; just two years earlier, she had helped lead a strike by shirtwaist workers, including those at the Triangle Shirtwaist Factory, only to see several of the largest companies—including Triangle—refuse to comply with demands.

As a result, many of the women engaged in that strike, standing elbow to elbow with Schneiderman, had met grisly deaths. Speaking forcefully and yet barely above a whisper, she told those assembled at the Opera House: "I would be a traitor to those poor burned bodies if I were to come here to talk good fellowship. We have tried you good people of the public," she said, pausing, "and we have found you wanting."

ROSE SCHNEIDERMAN

WE HAVE TRIED
YOU GOOD PEOPLE
OF THE PUBLIC—
AND WE HAVE
FOUND YOU
WANTING.

—ROSE SCHNEIDERMAN, 1911

Her blunt, searing appraisal of how those in power had failed the Triangle girls and numerous other workplace accident victims stunned the well-to-do audience.

Schneiderman would go on to help establish the International Ladies' Garment Workers' Union (ILGWU), develop a close friendship with Eleanor Roosevelt, and become a member of FDR's "braintrust" and an advisor to one of his New Deal agencies. She also served for six years (1937–1943) as secretary to the New York State Department of Labor.

Among those who were deeply moved by Schneiderman's declarations was **FRANCES PERKINS** (1880–1965), an ambitious reformer who seized the moment to begin work on what would eventually become some of the most progressive labor reform laws in the nation. Perkins grew up in Massachusetts, very much a daughter of loving "Downeasters" who had for generations farmed and operated a brickyard in rural Maine. She also enjoyed a close bond with a wise, widowed grandmother, who shared many stories about their family's Yankee history of self-sufficiency.

But it was while studying the rise of industrialism at Mount Holyoke College that Perkins—who had been taught that nice people were poor because of alcohol or laziness, a widely held viewpoint in that era—was forever changed by a visit to a mill in Connecticut. There she saw women and children enduring slave-like conditions, with no cap on mandatory hours, no safety measures, and no compensation should on-the-job injury render them unable to earn their keep. Because of this experience, Perkins, a devout Episcopalian, decided to dedicate herself to ameliorating such "unnecessary hazards to life," such "unnecessary poverty."

In 1909, she moved to New York City, where she took a job with the National Consumers League, an organization taking steps to limit work hours for children and adults, and to establish sanitary and safety regulations for the City's businesses. There, in 1911, Perkins, 31, was among the horrified crowd offering final witness to the Triangle workers jumping to their deaths. (She happened to be taking tea with friends at a townhouse in Washington Square but was drawn outside by the sound of fire trucks.) When in the aftermath of the tragedy a commission was established to recommend new safety regulations, Governor Al Smith appointed Perkins to lead it.

Unafraid to confront the abuses head-on, Perkins took legislators on tours of factories and worksites to show them firsthand the dangers of unfettered manufacturing. Those efforts helped produce the first (and most comprehensive) set of workplace health and safety laws in the nation.

When Franklin Delano Roosevelt became governor of New York in 1928, he promoted Perkins to oversee the entire New York labor department. He then turned to her for ideas about how to address the rising crisis of unemployment. Perkins soon expanded existing employment programs, organized conferences, and explored the prospect of unemployment insurance, even traveling to England to study the issue.

After FDR was elected to the Oval Office, he asked Perkins to join his cabinet as Secretary of Labor. Before accepting the appointment, Perkins wrote out the following goals—now widely considered a basic standard—and insisted that Roosevelt confirm in advance his full support of her vision: the establishment of a forty-hour work week, a minimum wage, abolishment of child labor, unemployment compensation, worker's compensation, social security, a revitalized federal employment service, and universal health care. With his agreement, Perkins became the first female in U.S. history to serve in a presidential cabinet (an occasion that led *The Atlanta Constitution* to take note of her "extraordinarily well-shaped hands"). With the exception of universal health insurance, which has kept politicians arguing well into the twenty-first century, in time, Perkins achieved all of her goals, thus revolutionizing the life of every American—especially the lives of the many low-level laborers in New York City.

Most significantly for New York, Perkins was also the creator and primary driver of what became the Works Progress Administration (WPA), the federal employment agency created as part of Roosevelt's New Deal to combat the Great Depression. By 1936, the federal government was spending $20 million a month in New York City alone. Mayor Fiorello H. La Guardia, taking advantage of the program, used WPA funds to rebuild and/or modernize many NYC sites, including La Guardia Airport, the Prospect Park Zoo, the entire lower section of FDR Drive, 255 playgrounds, and seventeen municipal swimming pools— not to mention repairs to thousands of miles of roads and hundreds of schools

THE DOOR MIGHT NOT BE OPENED

TO A WOMAN AGAIN FOR A LONG,

LONG TIME, AND I HAD A KIND OF

DUTY TO OTHER WOMEN TO WALK IN

AND SIT DOWN ON THE CHAIR THAT

WAS OFFERED, AND SO ESTABLISH

THE RIGHT OF OTHERS LONG HENCE

AND FAR DISTANT IN GEOGRAPHY TO

SIT IN THE HIGH SEATS.

—FRANCES PERKINS, 1945

and the refurbishment of countless hospitals and police and fire stations. In the process, these works provided much-needed employment for thousands of New Yorkers, from men toiling at the Brooklyn Navy Yard to the artists hired by the New Deal's Federal Arts Project (including the painter Jackson Pollock and photographer Berenice Abbott) to the young scribes (including John Cheever and Ralph Ellison) employed by the Federal Writers' Project.

In 1944, *Collier's* described Perkins's work over the previous twelve years as "not so much the Roosevelt New Deal as it is the Perkins New Deal."

Although Perkins married the economist Paul Caldwell Wilson in 1913, for many years Perkins lived in Washington, DC, with Mary Harriman Rumsey, a socialite whose political sympathies, financial support, and companionship were instrumental in Perkins's success. Today, her grandson, Tomlin Perkins Coggeshall, carries on Perkins's work through the Frances Perkins Center in Maine, which he founded in her honor.

In 1927, **ELLA BAKER** (1903–1986) moved from Raleigh, North Carolina, to New York City. A freshly minted valedictorian from historically black Shaw University, she brought with her a deep concern for fairness and a willingness to confront what she "considered contradictions in what was said and what was done."

She held a number of odd jobs, including stints at two Harlem newspapers, where she came into contact with leading black thinkers like George Schuyler, an important social critic. She also joined several community organizations and helped Schuyler start the Young Negroes Cooperative League (YNCL), an early grocery co-op that allowed black New Yorkers to pool funds to get better prices on food.

From her work at the YNCL, Baker became so adept at value purchasing that the Works Progress Administration (WPA) hired her to teach buying classes. In addition, Schuyler recognized her gifts in inspiring youth support for activist causes; at his encouragement, she toured the country, grew the ranks of YNCL, and motivated African Americans to participate in the democratic process.

Around 1940, Baker was hired by the National Association for the Advancement of Colored People (NAACP), which had been founded in Manhattan in 1909. An astute organizer and strategist, she began representing the NYC headquarters around the country, raising funds and recruiting members, eventually becoming the NAACP's national director of branches. In that post, she assisted with the creation of new chapters, helped local leaders organize grassroots campaigns—campaigns against lynching, for example, and for equal pay and job training—and provided leadership training to local figures, including Rosa Parks.

While the NAACP focused its resources on winning the battle for equality through the courts, Baker sensed that lasting change was more likely to emerge from daily life. Her next forum for creating change arose from her role,

beginning in 1957, as executive director of the Southern Christian Leadership Conference (SCLC), a position offered by Dr. Martin Luther King Jr. on behalf of several ministers set on mounting boycott campaigns throughout the South. Though she found the members' chauvinist attitudes (and relentless condescension) unpalatable, such didn't stop her from launching the organization—and a theretofore little-known King—onto a national stage.

But in February 1960, after four black college students in North Carolina refused to leave a Woolworth's lunch counter when they were denied service, Baker left the SCLC to assist the new student activists. She soon organized an event out of which was born the Student Nonviolent Coordinating Committee (SNCC; pronounced "snick"), which proved to be one of the most important groups behind the 1960s civil rights movement.

Though she spent the majority of her time raising awareness and publicizing her cause, Baker herself was almost never in front of the camera. For one thing, she never sought fame; but also, the pervasive sexism of the day—embodied in Stokely Carmichael's infamous joke that "the only position for women in SNCC is prone"—meant public leadership positions were usually denied to women. That Baker persevered and ultimately succeeded within this environment makes her a symbol of resilience; and though she faced gender oppression even within her ranks, during her life she nonetheless earned the nickname "Fundi," a Swahili word for someone who passes craft down to the next generation. In the end, despite the fact that, or perhaps because, her grandmother had endured the dehumanizing violation of slavery, Baker played a pivotal role in all of the most important civil rights groups of her era. As such, she deserves recognition as the City's—and the country's—first lady of civil rights.

Despite the significant gains in racial equality that Baker helped achieve, she and other female leaders often noted that gender could be an even more fraught component of identity than race or ethnicity.

In 1963, Ohio-born **GLORIA STEINEM** (b. 1934), a graduate of Smith College, having gone undercover as a waitress/"bunny" at a newly opened Playboy Club in Manhattan, described the experience in a two-part series for *Show* magazine.

A few years later, she covered a speak-out organized by the Redstockings, a radical feminist group, to protest the fact that the New York State Legislature, when considering a liberalization of abortion law, invited to testify fourteen men and one woman—a nun. With this incident she experienced an awakening of her feminist consciousness, as it brought her to realize just how outraged she was by the injustices experienced by women. "It was the first time in my life I had heard women standing up in public and talking about something that you weren't supposed to talk about, and that only happened to women—and taking it seriously," she told me. "Suddenly I understood the politics of sexism in the deep sense: that it was about controlling reproduction and therefore women's bodies."

In clear, calm prose, Steinem began using the political column she wrote for the newly launched *New York* magazine to directly advocate for women's rights. Taking the many sexist experiences she and other female city-dwellers encountered on a daily basis, she pushed to make her concerns part of the national conversation. In 1970, she delivered a commencement address at Vassar College entitled "Living the Revolution." She told the students: "Our first problem is not to learn but to unlearn, to clear out some of the old assumptions: patriotism means obedience, age means wisdom, black means inferior, woman means submission. They just don't work anymore."

Attractive and articulate, and speaking truths that many women had until then only privately endured, Steinem quickly became the face of what is commonly considered the "second wave" of the American feminism movement. She also embraced the popular rallying slogan of the era, "the personal is political," and coined the phrase "reproductive freedom."

In 1970, she testified before the U.S. Senate about the necessity of the Equal Rights Amendment. The following year, she published (with Dorothy Pitman Hughes and six founding editors) *Ms.* magazine, the country's first national glossy periodical produced and operated by women. Initially packaged as an insert to *New York*, the three-hundred-thousand printing sold out in eight days, launching a groundbreaking monthly that is still in operation today.

In 1973, Steinem joined with Patricia Carbine, Letty Cottin Pogrebin, and Marlo Thomas to create the Ms. Foundation for Women, which funded domestic violence shelters and sexual-assault hotlines, created programs for women's economic development and sex education, organized groups to work for reproductive rights and social justice, and in 1993 introduced Take Our Daughters to Work Day, a widely successful national public education campaign that was expanded a decade later to include boys. In 2005 she cofounded (with Jane Fonda and Robin Morgan) the Women's Media Center, an organization dedicated to making women more visible and powerful in the media.

For decades Steinem has lectured on feminist issues, lent support to student and feminist groups, and tried to bring attention to the distinct needs of women of color. For example, when, by dint of her celebrity, she was invited to speak around the country, she nearly always brought along a speaking partner, like the black feminist Florynce "Flo" Kennedy, or civil rights trailblazer Dorothy Pitman Hughes. Steinem has organized numerous benefits, given her time to various political organizations, and made many appearances on television.

Overall, her advocacy has had an immeasurable impact on women's rights in New York, from which it spread to the rest of the country and—it isn't an overstatement to say—the world. Still publishing and advocating and mentoring younger activists in her eighth decade, this *fundi*—like Ella Baker, someone who passes craft down to the next generation—spent 2014, the year of her eightieth birthday, as she said, "using myself" to promote feminist causes, offering a message that could be New York City's mantra: "The future depends entirely on what each of us does every day."

WALL STREET

In 2016, a former managing director at Bear Stearns revealed in *The New York Times* that male colleagues had welcomed her to Wall Street with a pizza studded with unwrapped condoms, proving that the work of civilizing men on Wall Street is an unfinished process.

But imagine how much further away civility would be if it weren't for VICTORIA WOODHULL (1838–1927). In 1870, Victoria and her younger sister, Tennessee "Tennie" Claflin, opened a brokerage firm on Wall Street (backed by funds from Cornelius Vanderbilt). This was half a century before women were even guaranteed the right to vote.

Upon opening shop at 44 Broad Street, Woodhull sent pretty much the entire financial district—not to mention the City's male-dominated newsrooms—into a dither.

Bankers and traders, unable to stop themselves from gawking at such exotic specimens, flocked to the firm's storefront window to take a gander, or joined a long line of those keen on actually meeting them. Some fellows even gussied up beforehand, donning their dandiest finery.

Woodhull was a relative newcomer to New York, and she had arrived with a checkered past. After surviving an unstable childhood in Ohio, she married at fifteen, divorced, and then reinvented herself—first in the theater in San

Francisco, next becoming a traveling "medical clairvoyant." But her possession of generous measures of gumption put her on par with the era's other financial speculators, and the firm quickly made a bundle.

Simultaneously, Woodhull became a devotee of Stephen Pearl Andrews, an abolitionist phonography expert and radical philosopher who espoused a philosophy of individualist utopia, leading her to decide her true quest was to help women achieve financial and sexual freedom.

In 1871 she launched a newspaper, *Woodhull and Claflin's Weekly*; the same year, she became the first woman in history to address a committee of the U.S. Congress. She was also the first person in America to publish an English translation of *The Communist Manifesto*.

In 1872, at age thirty-three, she announced her candidacy for U.S. president, becoming the first woman ever to make a run for the White House.

Prominent suffragists like Susan B. Anthony were initially thrilled to welcome an attractive, outspoken, attention-seeking addition to the cause; but when, at an important suffrage convention, Woodhull tried to shift focus off of the singular goal of enfranchisement to a wider platform of political issues, they would repudiate her, and all but omit her from their landmark accounts of feminist history.

Still, Woodhull was the first to blaze the path, and it wasn't until the panic of 1907 that another woman would affect the financial sector in such a significant way.

After stock prices plummeted and investors unloaded billions of dollars in securities, two financial firms declared bankruptcy, setting off a run on the banks.

With another firm on the brink of collapse, **HETTY GREEN**, (1834–1916), one of New York's wealthiest investors, promptly loaned $1.1 million to the City and millions more to individuals and banks, thereby helping to stabilize the market.

Despite a reputation for being a miser—which in many ways she was—Green was already the City's largest lender: according to a 1930 biography, the City repeatedly turned to Green for low-interest loans, including one for $4.5 million.

Green's vast wealth was achieved after her father's death, when she inherited an estimated one million dollars. Having started reading commodities reports to her father when she was only six, Green should have been known as the "Oracle of Wall Street": she astutely maneuvered the markets and became one of the richest people in the world, worth an estimated $100 to $200 million (the modern day equivalent of at least $2.2 billion). Upon marrying in 1867, she insisted on keeping her funds separate and under her own control; after her husband later risked some of her money without permission, she paid off his debts and left him.

Green was widely derided in the press for being miserly (she eschewed new clothes and rented in Hoboken to avoid NYC property tax) and for her habit of dressing in a heavy black dress and veil. But she had grown up in a Quaker home that valued thrift, and began wearing a veil after the death of her husband (from whom she never legally divorced).

Instead of being lauded as one of the foremost financial wizards in history, Hetty Green is usually remembered, unfairly and absurdly, as "The Witch of Wall Street."

In 1967, half a century after Green died in 1916, **MURIEL SIEBERT** (1928–2013) earned a more meaningful title upon purchasing a seat on the New York Stock Exchange. How so? At the time, all 1,365 members of the exchange were men.

Despite a predictable onslaught of hazing (including a headline that read "Skirt Invades Exchange," a modernized version of an editorial published upon Woodhull's arrival to the Street more than a century earlier, which read "Vive la froufrou!"), Siebert opened her own financial firm called Muriel Siebert & Co., and in 1975, when laws eliminated fixed commission rates for brokers, she transformed her company into one of the nation's first discount brokerages.

While most Wall Street banks were bastions of male dominance, Siebert, who was known as "Mickie," attracted a steady stream of female customers, many who needed sound advice after having been manipulated by greedy men.

In 1977, Governor Hugh Carey asked Siebert to become the state's superintendent of banking. Under her leadership, not a single banking institution failed.

Eventually the "First Woman of Finance" would direct her comfort with mathematics into creating a personal finance program for middle and high school students.

A 2002 autobiography urged women to blaze whatever paths necessary to reach their professional goals, and revealed the habits of thinking that led to her success: "Lead, follow, or get the hell out of the way."

HETTY GREEN, "THE WITCH OF WALL STREET"

THE BENEFACTORS

While her husband, John D. Rockefeller Jr., was busy being heir to the Standard Oil fortune, **ABBY ALDRICH ROCKEFELLER** (1874–1948) found ways to support progressive causes like the YWCA and the American Birth Control League (ABCL), the forerunner of Planned Parenthood. She served as chair of an American Red Cross Auxiliary, dedicating space in her home to prepare thousands of "comfort bags" for soldiers on fighting fronts abroad, and chaired a YWCA committee to build quality housing for working women.

She also collected art that was considered experimental or, in the words of her husband, "unintelligible"; possessing a sophisticated sense of aesthetics, she amassed a collection of work by then-unknowns like Georgia O'Keeffe, Vincent van Gogh, Diego Rivera, Henri Matisse, and Pablo Picasso, which were displayed on an upper floor of the family's townhouse on West 54th Street. After the 1913 Armory Show, the first significant showing of modern work in the United States, several prominent members of the City discussed establishing a museum for modern art—but no one took the initiative to do anything about it until Abby Aldrich Rockefeller resolved otherwise.

As her darling husband didn't approve of using their resources to show "indiscernible dreck" to the masses, Rockefeller joined with two friends in raising funds for the project. As the result, the Museum of Modern Art (MoMA), the first museum in the country devoted to the modern movement, opened in 1929.

During the museum's first decade Rockefeller provided what a biographer called "visionary management"—as well as the institution's first formal purchase funds. She held various positions at what her family affectionately referred to as "Mother's museum," including member of the board of trustees.

To honor Rockefeller's contributions, the Abby Aldrich Rockefeller Sculpture Garden, designed by Philip Johnson, was dedicated two years after her death in 1948. Her influence was still felt half a century later when, by decree of her will, MoMA transferred to other museums several valuable impressionistic works she had originally donated. The reason? Always a farsighted thinker, she had believed that, in time, those works would no longer be "modern."

At the dawn of the twentieth century, **GERTRUDE VANDERBILT WHITNEY** (1875–1942) began studying sculpture, both at the Art Students League of New York and, for a period, in Paris, where she visited with Auguste Rodin. She then became an active part of the bohemian Greenwich Village art scene, purchasing a studio on MacDougal Alley, organizing exhibits for fellow artists, and, in 1918, establishing the Whitney Studio Club, a place where young local artists could hang out, play billiards, and utilize the facility's reference library or sketch room.

Throughout this time, Whitney came into contact with numerous young artists, whose work she avidly collected. (As she was a great-granddaughter of shipping and railroad magnate "Commodore" Cornelius Vanderbilt and the wife of a member of the prominent Whitney family, money was plentiful.) By 1929, in addition to becoming a successful sculptor in her own right, she had amassed more than five hundred works by the likes of then-unknowns such as Max Weber, Reginald Marsh, and Edward Hopper. Believing American modernists deserved greater recognition, she offered to donate them (with an endowment) to the Metropolitan Museum of Art. But after the traditional-minded Met declined the offer, she instead founded the Whitney Museum of American Art, which opened in 1931 on West 8th Street.

The following year, she organized what today remains the preeminent show-case for emerging American artists: the Whitney Annual Exhibition. (After it shifted to a biennial schedule in 1973, it became known as the Whitney Biennial.) Whereas most museums have no regular schedule for obtaining new work, Ms. Whitney utilized the recurring event as a forum for regularly continually growing her collection, thereby establishing the Whitney—and by extension, New York City—as perpetually on the cutting edge of American modern art.

⁜　　⁜

In the annals of philanthropy, no socialite could ever mean more to New York than **BROOKE ASTOR** (1902–2007), the City's grand dame of high society

who, throughout the second half of the twentieth century, provided financial support for many of its most beloved cultural institutions, including the New York Public Library, the Bronx Zoo, and the Metropolitan Museum of Art.

Astor's third husband, Vincent Astor, was heir to the fortune of John Jacob Astor IV, a fur magnate and financier who went down with the RMS *Titanic* in 1912. Upon Vincent's death in 1959, Brooke Astor became president of his foundation and began the work of giving away its money.

But, unlike most society ladies before her, Astor parlayed her adept social and intellectual abilities into a new kind of philanthropic leadership. She showed up in person wherever she was donating—wearing her trademark pearls and elegant suits—which sent the message that kindergartens in the Bronx were as much a part of the City as the NYPL.

Astor funded countless small projects as well, like chess tables in parks; construction of the George Washington Carver Houses in East Harlem (along with its brick outdoor amphitheaters); fire escapes for a homeless residence in the Bronx; and free care for pets of indigent seniors. When she died at 105 in 2007, *The New York Times* noted the personal creed that rightly earned the headline "Aristocrat of the People" on her obituary: "I grew up feeling that the most important thing in life was to have good manners and to enhance the lives of others."

BROOKE ASTOR

THE FUNDER

By the time the nineteenth century gave way to the twentieth, the great epidemics of smallpox, cholera, and yellow fever had ended. Tuberculosis, however, remained rampant among the City's poor, as did childhood diseases like diphtheria, measles, dysentery, and whooping cough. And though public health was in its infancy, it didn't take much for physicians and researchers to identify a major source of the problem: lack of hygiene.

In teeming slums on the Lower East Side, poor immigrant families—often with five, six, even ten children—were packed into one or two small rooms with no ventilation and little or no access to running water. (In 1900, thirty-nine tenement buildings on one block were found to house a total of 2,781 people, who shared just forty taps with hot running water and 264 water closets.) The scarcity of taps meant that bathing was inconvenient and cumbersome—and therefore rarely performed. And with water closets being far from sanitary, disease-carrying bacteria quickly made its way from family to family.

Enter **ELIZABETH MILBANK ANDERSON** (1850–1921), who, in 1884, inherited half her father Jeremiah Milbank's enormous fortune, which he had amassed as a railroad magnate and as an owner of what became the

Borden Condensed Milk Company. Given her devotion to her Baptist parents, Elizabeth used her family's name for all of her philanthropic work in the City.

Anderson, who lost her only son to diphtheria in 1886, was convinced that health was at the foundation of human happiness. And so, she sought means by which she could help prevent others from suffering. When she became involved with the Association for Improving the Condition of the Poor (AICP), she learned of the plight of fellow New Yorkers lacking access to facilities for basic hygiene. While most affluent philanthropists funded projects that would display their largesse—a museum or a monument—Anderson instead donated funds to build a public bath. Her gift would become a model for the City, as it established the groundwork for hygiene being practiced as the very foundation of public health.

When the Milbank Memorial People's Bath opened on East 38th Street in 1904, it was one of just two or three places where the City's poor could bathe—and it could accommodate three thousand bathers in a single day. It was divided into separate sections for men and women and also provided a space for washing clothes. Images from the period show filthy children, many without shoes, crowded onto the building's stairs, waiting for their turn to go inside. Needless to say, the facility greatly transformed tens of thousands of city-dwellers' lives.

In addition to addressing sanitation, Anderson sought to strengthen children's health through the provision of meals to 25,000 students in New York City public elementary schools.

Anderson's good works didn't end there. In 1905 she created what is now known as The Milbank Memorial Fund, endowing it with $9.3 million. The foundation became a major private source of funds for public health and social and preventive medicine through the twentieth century. By creating a facility with Anne Harriman Vanderbilt where infected patients and their families could convalesce—The Home Hospital for the Tubercular—the fund helped NYC greatly reduce annual deaths from tuberculosis, which in 1910 had numbered over ten thousand.

To further help children, in 1909, Anderson provided one million dollars to the Children's Aid Society for the purchase, renovation, and operation of the Chappaqua Mountain Institute as a sanitarium for ill and crippled children. From 1912 until 1922, the "Home For Convalescent Children" provided care to 7,903 boys and girls of impoverished urban families recovering from a variety of diseases.

Anderson had also been a major benefactor and trustee of Barnard, a women's college founded in 1889 that operated out of a rented brownstone at 343 Madison Avenue. In 1896, she funded the construction of its own building, "Milbank Hall," a red brick structure on a plot between 119th and 120th Streets, bound by Broadway and Claremont Avenue. Then, in 1903 she anonymously purchased the adjoining three city blocks stretching south all the way to 116th Street; her deeding it to the school ensured Barnard would have an adequate campus.

In none of these places throughout the City where her support was so instrumental can the name ELIZABETH MILBANK ANDERSON be found; she always opted instead for simply the Milbank family name. But her (perhaps) modesty aside, her determination to fund projects that would have a lasting effect on New Yorkers' quality of life—and the advancement of the City—lives on.

THE AMBASSADOR

After making her social debut, **ELEANOR ROOSEVELT** (1884-1962), a descendant of the City's earliest Dutch settlers and a granddaughter of Theodore Roosevelt Sr., was inspired by how her friend, the debutante Mary Harriman, utilized her life of privilege to found The Junior League, a group initially devoted to supporting the Settlement House movement. She decided she likewise wanted to do more with her life than attend parties. The teen-aged Roosevelt began by teaching dance and calisthenics, then believed to improve health after long hours working in a confined space, at the College Settlement House on Rivington Street. She also worked at The Consumer's League, where she investigated and documented the conditions of tenement sweatshops where people lived and worked.

After meeting Franklin Delano Roosevelt, a fifth cousin once removed, during a train ride up the Hudson River, they began a clandestine courtship; in 1905, when she was twenty and he was twenty-two, they married.

For about a decade and a half, Roosevelt served as a dutiful political wife—first in Albany and then in Washington, where FDR served as Secretary of the Navy under Woodrow Wilson. She gave birth to the couple's six children, losing one in infancy.

When FDR contracted polio, Roosevelt initially oversaw his medical care, but once a secretary was employed to take over household management duties, Roosevelt was freed to pursue her own interests. These included joining The Women's City Club of New York, for which she would make radio broadcasts on current political issues and become part of the organization's leadership, and the Women's Trade Union League, which helped female garment industry laborers unionize and advocate for fair wages and work hours. She also joined the League of Women Voters, became the newsletter editor and columnist for the Women's Division of the New York State Democratic Committee, worked for a variety of publications as a freelance journalist, and, according to the National First Ladies' Library, created a committee to judge a contest in which competitors submitted plans to create world peace.

When FDR returned to Albany as Governor in 1929, Roosevelt quit most of her political groups but continued making her "Women in Politics" radio broadcast, remaining home in Manhattan half of her time. She also began utilizing her position as the governor's wife to influence state politics, successfully encouraging FDR to reform employment and labor programs that directly affected the life of workers in the City.

Upon becoming First Lady of the United States in 1933, Roosevelt, then forty-eight, decided to continue her work as a writer, public speaker, and media figure, and began leveraging her platform to promote the reform causes to which she had always been devoted. To force news organizations to employ female scribes, she held regular press conferences from which she barred male reporters.

She also began writing monthly columns for various women's magazines, and beginning in 1935, she penned a syndicated, six-day-a-week newspaper column called "My Day," in which she encouraged women to develop talents and interests outside traditional roles and advocated for progressive causes like civil rights. She famously used one column to explain her resignation from the Daughters of the American Revolution for its refusal to permit Marian Anderson, the acclaimed African American contralto singer, to perform.

She wrote numerous lengthy magazine articles about the moral necessity of civil rights, published books, and gave an estimated 1,400 speeches on a variety of progressive causes.

Roosevelt spent an unprecedented three terms in the White House, during which time she routinely spoke out on civil rights for all, refused to soften her stance for political expediency (even letting it be known publicly that she disapproved of the decision by her husband's administration of interning Japanese Americans after the Pearl Harbor attack), invited a wide array of artists into the White House, and, upon seeing the dearth of opportunities available to workers in the New Hyde area where the Roosevelt family owned homes, she joined with friends and opened a factory to put local people to work.

Over the twenty-two years of her life after leaving the White House, Roosevelt worked with the NAACP, participated in the creation of a Civil Rights Division within the Justice department, fundraised with Martin Luther King Jr. and Rosa Parks for participants in civil disobedience, lobbied to make permanent the outlawing of racial discrimination in federal employment

MY VOICE WILL
NOT BE SILENT.

—ELEANOR ROOSEVELT, 1945

(after having earlier convinced FDR to issue a similar Executive Order), co-chaired a fundraiser for striking union members, supported the Equal Rights Amendment, and testified before Congress to support legislation guaranteeing gender pay equity.

Roosevelt remade the post of the country's first lady. But it was her modeling of a humanist spirit—routinely defending the underdog, picking up the downtrodden, believing in the equality of all races, demonstrating the value of the arts to society and individuals, and repeatedly choosing to devote her time to substantive matters over fluff (she would even, upon finding a dress she liked, order it in several colors to avoid devoting more time to fittings)—that made her a symbol of New York.

Her spirit reflected a New Yorker's sensibility and the melting pot ethos—as such she was poised to become the first true citizen of the world. In 1945, she was appointed by President Harry Truman to serve as one of five delegates to the newly formed United Nations, where she successfully promoted a variety of American proposals and advocated for oppressed and tyrannized people worldwide. With decades of writing and editing experience, she took on the formidable task of drafting the first ever-attempted Universal Declaration of Human Rights, an effort that required months of difficult political negotiations between representatives from countries with widely divergent cultures and beliefs.

On December 10, 1948, as Human Rights Commission chair, Eleanor presented the declaration to the U.N. General Assembly, and in a historic moment for all people devoted to freedom and social justice, the declaration was ratified.

The document remains the principal guide the world over to assess a government's treatment of its people. And it established Roosevelt's place as the ultimate New Yorker.

MADISON AVENUE

In the 1960s the phrase "Madison Avenue" became shorthand for the powerful multibillion-dollar advertising industry that drove the fortunes of most American industries and helped to create what came to be known as popular culture. But the role of the advertising industry in promulgating the gospel of consumerism actually began in the 1920s, when American factories transitioned from producing munitions to making a vast array of household appliances and automobiles. In this environment, advertisers needed to do more than just sell products—they also had to devise strategies for creating new markets of people to buy them.

Not surprisingly, most professionals involved in that endeavor were men. But, one night in 1911, **CHRISTINE FREDERICK** (1883–1970), a housewife whose husband worked at the ad agency J. Walter Thompson, found herself fascinated when a business friend of her husband visited their Bronx apartment to discuss topics like "efficiency," "standard practice," and "scientific management."

Frederick asked the guest to visit again and tell her more. From subsequent conversations, she quickly absorbed the logic of Taylorism, a late-nineteenth-century system of evaluating every step in manufacturing so as to increase productivity. An immediate convert, she decided to apply this system to the domestic sphere, which she personally found "drudgifying."

Through a series of articles for *Ladies' Home Journal* entitled "The New Housekeeping," she applied the scientific language of efficiency to domestic life, encouraging readers to minimize physical routes between essential locations in the kitchen, to ensure necessary equipment is readily accessible, and, as a means of better maintaining a clean, happy home, to buy "every device she can afford."

Next she moved her family to Long Island, where in 1900 she founded the Applecroft Home Experiment Station, a product-evaluation laboratory similar to the Good Housekeeping Institute. At Applecroft she tested a wide variety of devices, then sold her reviews as advertising copy—all the while using her editorial writings (which grew to include two books and a syndicated newspaper column) to push housewives to think of themselves as family "purchasing agents."

Over the next decade, Frederick became widely known as a consumer advocate and home-efficiency expert, and she simultaneously worked as a consultant to advertisers. So as to give females a greater voice in the ad industry, in 1912 she and her husband established the League of Advertising Women of New York (now Advertising Women of New York, Inc., or AWNY). But it was her landmark 1929 book, *Selling Mrs. Consumer,* that brought sales and advertising types to first recognize the importance of women to the consumer economy; this in turn provided the roadmap for Madison Avenue to promote the idea of buying products (for one's family) as an act of familial devotion—even patriotism.

Although Frederick seemed blithely unaware of the eventual environmental and social implications of the mass consumerism she preached, she was instrumental in not only validating consumerism in the eyes of American women, but also building the idea in American minds that buying "things" was a social, moral—and even maternal—good, a condition on which Madison Avenue's survival (not to mention a significant part of the U.S. economy) would depend in the coming decades.

As a young newlywed, alone in New York while her husband fought in WWII, **EILEEN FORD** (1922–2014) had spent about two years doing assorted jobs in the fashion industry when, in 1946, she became the secretary of a friend, the model Natalie Nickerson.

Tasked with the administrative work of preparing for photo shoots and afterward collecting fees, Ford tackled the job with aplomb; soon she also booked Nickerson on new assignments. Word of her talents spread among Nickerson's modeling friends, many of whom disliked how their male agents often sent them to fend for themselves in scary situations and weren't particularly concerned when they weren't paid. In short order, Ford found herself with about a dozen clients willing to pay $65 a month for her assistance.

In the following year her husband, Jerry, returned from service, and she gave birth to their first child. By then, business was booming. Taking the leap to officially establish the Ford Modeling Agency, they used the proceeds from selling their car to pay rent on a small walk-up office on Second Avenue, where Ford quickly began imposing order on the chaotic industry.

First, she and Jerry established a fixed billing and payment system. Next she set clear standards about what she would—and would not—allow her models to do; for example, no ads for bras or deodorant, no bathtubs, no "excessive amounts of bosom."

Unlike most agents at the time, Ford, who had exacting standards and a strong vision of how her models should look, became personally involved in her models' lives, giving them advice on clothing, hair, and makeup. (Later she augmented her advice with a Rolodex full of dermatologists, nutritionists, and hairdressers.) But her consult wasn't always in the models' favor: she bluntly told those who stayed up all night partying that they wouldn't remain in her employment.

Ford's vision of what a model should look like—tall, blonde, glamorous, fresh but not aloof; a preternaturally beautiful (and Caucasian) all-American girl next door—set the standard for models and, consequently, for fashion as a whole. She also discovered some of the twentieth century's most famous faces, including Lauren Hutton, Christie Brinkley, Rachel Hunter, Kim Basinger, Carol Alt, and Christy Turlington.

Overall, her professionalization of the modeling industry led to New York becoming the ultimate destination for models, laying the groundwork for the unprecedented level of fame supermodels like Cindy Crawford reached in the 1980s, the era when fashion magazines first began routinely putting celebrities on covers.

EILEEN FORD

OF COURSE, I'M A
LEGEND. BUT IT'S
NOT BECAUSE OF
ANY GREAT GIFT
I HAVE. I'M A
RISK TAKER.

—MARY WELLS LAWRENCE, 2002

Of course, there's no question that Ford's vision of female perfection contributed to the harmful idealization of white beauty standards and the scourge of perfectionism. All the same, prior to Ford's transformation of the industry, models were regularly exploited. As Lauren Hutton told Ford biographer Robert Lacey, she was "a cloak to us": "She threw a huge cloak of safety over the girls in her care—and that made her, in my book, a great changer for the sake of women."

When the English poet and playwright William Congreve wrote in 1697 that hell has no "fury like a woman scorned," he was unlikely to have imagined the moment in 1966 when **MARY WELLS LAWRENCE** (b. 1928), a highly respected copywriter at Jack Tinker & Partners, was offered a $1 million contract paid over ten years to be essentially the authority of the president of the agency—though she would not hold that title.

"It's not my fault, Mary," she recalls the agency's owner telling her. "The world is not ready for women presidents." Indignant, she marched out of the office and soon thereafter opened what quickly became the hottest agency on Madison Avenue, Wells Rich Greene. By the end of its first year, the firm had one hundred employees and $30 million in billings.

With legendary bravado and influence, Wells Lawrence helped to create the image of New York as a den of powerbrokers. She also produced an array of clever, innovative means of selling products that revolutionized the industry, such as presenting television commercials as mini-movies or, to quote the Advertising Hall of Fame, as "sixty seconds of visual entertainment with the product as the star."

Her firm created some of television's most memorable campaigns, including Alka-Seltzer's "Plop, Plop, Fizz, Fizz" and Ford Motor Company's "Quality Is Job One." She also produced remarkable results for her clients; when she introduced spots stating that two Alka-Seltzer tablets were even better than one, sales of the digestive remedy immediately doubled.

In an industry where the most powerful men tended to work behind the scenes—and yes, they were all men—Wells Lawrence put herself out front, pushing her staff to come up with even fresher ideas, outmaneuvering other firms in the process. "Mary was to Madison Avenue what Muhammad Ali was to boxing," said Charlie Moss, the first writer she hired.

The excitement surrounding her work became a catalyst for the widespread creative boom the entire industry experienced in the 1960s, which ultimately led Madison Avenue to become a primary engine of the economy and American popular culture. It also led to Wells Lawrence becoming the first female CEO of a company listed on the New York Stock Exchange.

The legacy she built for New York City, however, didn't just include its identity as a destination for the best and the brightest; it also became a lasting form of economic stability. In the wake of the City's near-bankruptcy in the 1970s, Wells Lawrence accepted the assignment, free of charge, of figuring out how to tap into NYC's untapped potential for tourism. Armed with research indicating that New York inspired a range of emotions for people everywhere, Wells Lawrence spearheaded the team that created what became known as the "I Love New York" campaign, which put millions of dollars in the City's coffers and turned graphic designer Milton Glaser's "I ♥ NY" into an everlasting icon known throughout the world.

   "I defy you to find someone who's had a better life than me," Wells Lawrence, still swinging at seventy-three years old, told the reporter Bruce Horovitz in 2002. "I'll eat 'em."

HOT STUFF

As the nineteenth century gave way to the twentieth, several women drop-kicked aside old notions of a "fairer" sex, and, channeling their inner Aphrodites (and their Henry Fords), built new opportunities in Manhattan for human desire to flourish and, ahem, find satisfaction.

By the time eighteen-year-old Brooklyn-born **MAE WEST** (1893–1980) landed her first role on Broadway in 1911, she had already spent several years performing burlesque on the vaudeville circuit. Recognizing the appeal of her sexually coy characters, West embraced the image of a wanton sexpot, turning it into a public persona. She unabashedly shared with the press the highs and lows of a passionate and tumultuous love affair with a fellow vaudevillian, whether that meant passionate kisses on the street or full-fledged screaming matches. In 1918, when the Shubert brothers (Lee and J.J.) cast her in their revue *Sometime*, she scandalized and mesmerized audiences by performing the Jazz Age equivalent of Janet Jackson showing her nipple during the 2004 Super Bowl halftime show: dancing the shimmy, shoulders back, bosom forward.

Capitalizing on her growing renown as a sexual siren, West began altering scripts to amplify her characters' vivaciousness, crafting a string of double entendres that elevated the coy to the brazen. By 1926 she starred in her

own show, entitled *Sex*, which she also produced and directed. It packed the house for nearly a year before police got around to raiding the theater, jailing West and her entire company and charging them with lewdness and the corruption of the morals of youth. The ensuing trial and West's exoneration did wonders for publicity—and cemented New York's bawdy reputation in the bargain.

In 1925, a year before *Sex* debuted on Broadway for mainstream audiences, Eva Kotchever (1891–1943), a gender-bending Polish Jewish immigrant who went by the name **EVE ADAMS**, staked out a space for sexual freethinking in Greenwich Village. There, at 129 MacDougal Street, she opened Eve's Hangout, a tearoom where lesbian and bi-curious women could openly discuss radical politics and sexual identity.

Behind a front door with a facetious sign that read: MEN ARE ADMITTED, BUT NOT WELCOME, Adams, whose birth name was Chava Zloczower, created what amounted to one of the earliest lesbian bars in NYC, hosting poetry readings, musical performances, and late-night discussions that began the City's tradition of openly celebrating human sexuality in all its permutations. (According to the playwright Barbara Kahn, who researched Adams for several plays, she was an

I GENERALLY AVOID TEMPTATION, UNLESS I CAN'T RESIST IT.

—MAE WEST, 1940

early promoter of the work of Henry Miller and Anaïs Nin.) Many of the neighborhood's prominent poets, writers, and artists liked to stop by.

Admirers referred to Adams as "queen of the third sex"; detractors called her a "man-hater." During a police crackdown in the Village the following year, Adams unknowingly showed an undercover agent a collection of short stories she'd written and self-published for friends entitled "Lesbian Love"; she was promptly arrested, accused of making a homosexual advance toward the officer, and sentenced to a year and a half in the women's penitentiary on Blackwell's Island.

During her time behind bars, she met another inmate who'd been charged with similar offenses: Mae West. But whereas West's celebrity status freed her after just seven days, Adams had no such exit ticket and served her entire sentence.

Once released, Adams was deported to Poland, despite pleading to authorities that she should be allowed to stay. "I love this country with my whole heart and soul," she said at her hearing. "I want to become a citizen."

She spent the 1930s in Paris working as a bookseller, but in 1940, the Nazi invasion drove her south to Nice. Soon thereafter, she was arrested and, in 1943, forced on a train to Auschwitz, where she was promptly murdered.

In 1974, Dell Williams dared to open Eve's Garden, the nation's first sex shop catering specifically towards women—on the upper floor of an office building on West 57th Street. Had Eve Adams not created a safe space for women to undertake the historically radical act of exploring their sexual feelings half a century before, this step may not have been possible. Eve Adams succeeded in creating a space for women to undertake the historically radical act of safely exploring their sexual feelings.

⚜ ⚜

In the same decade Adams opened her tearoom, a Russian woman uptown set out with a comparatively banal objective: to become the "best goddamn madam in all America."

POLLY ADLER (1900–1962), who faced a series of tragic hardships after emigrating alone as a child from Russia in 1914, considered herself lucky when a bootlegger named Tony offered to pay her rent at a new private, Riverside Drive apartment—as long as she occasionally allowed him to meet there with his married lover. Both impoverished and laissez-faire about the concept of sex as a commodity—she later wrote that "whatever men are willing to pay for, someone will provide"—she began "finding" women for Tony and his friends. She earned $100 a week for her efforts—far more than she'd earned working at a factory.

As word spread and a steady stream of eager gals sought out her cash-flush connections, Adler grew her business. In 1924 she moved to what would become her best-remembered brothel, the Majestic on West 75th Street. She furnished the living room with plush furniture, creating a "clubhouse" feeling; "Going to Polly's" became what author Karen Abbott described as "the preferred late-night activity for the City's haut monde: gangsters Charles 'Lucky' Luciano and Dutch

Schultz, boxer Jack Dempsey, Mayor Jimmy Walker, and members of the Algonquin Round Table, including Dorothy Parker and Robert Benchley." Since regulars came to socialize as much or if not more than to visit the boudoir, revenue streamed to the "Queen of Tarts," as Adler became known, not only from the girls but also from sales of bootleg liquor.

For nearly twenty years, Adler ran a string of brothels throughout Manhattan; her business card—featuring a parrot on a perch—bore a seemingly upscale East Side exchange: Lexington 2-1099. And though she was repeatedly arrested as a "keeper of disorderly houses," her mastery of palming cash to cops in the local precinct—not to mention the hidden stairways and secret doors guests employed during police raids—went a long way in keeping her from prosecution. As she said herself, "I am one of those people who just can't help getting a kick out of life—even when it's a kick in the teeth."

THE NEWS MAKERS

When she was eighteen years old, **JANE GRANT** (1892–1972) was hired at *The New York Times*—though, as she later wrote in "Confession of a Feminist" in *The American Mercury*, she was "charged not to reveal the fact that a female had been hired" and was warned "there would never be advancement for a woman at the *Times*." In World War I, she went to Europe to entertain troops; while in France she met newspaper writer Harold Ross. They continued their friendship once back in New York—when Grant was made full-fledged reporter—and joined the group of writers, artists, and actors who became known as the "Algonquin Round Table" on account of their frequent merry-making sessions at the Algonquin Hotel, where they swapped ideas, collaborated on creative projects, and traded witticisms and barbs. (It was in part for this last reason that they were also known as the "Vicious Circle.")

Grant and Ross also developed a romance; though they privately married in 1920, they agreed to continue their independent careers—an uncommon stance for the era. Although Ross was known to privately grumble about it to friends on occasion, he also agreed that Grant would keep her own name, and that they would continue living with a revolving door of friends and colleagues.

It was at a meeting of the Vicious Circle that Ross, a shy, gangly Midwesterner, threw out the idea of starting a magazine. Even though most in the circle didn't think he could do it—and unabashedly delivered that verdict—Grant had other opinions, and took it upon herself to make the magazine a reality.

Prodding him into action, she suggested they live off only her earnings and set aside as seed money his $10,000 salary as editor of a magazine for veterans, *The Home Sector.* Then she encouraged Ross to ask his poker buddy Raoul Fleischmann (heir to his family's baking fortune) to contribute to the venture. All the while, Grant presided over the riot of humorists, writers, and literati who hung around, dined, and sometimes resided in their Hell's Kitchen home, a clubhouse of sorts where the group helped hatch plans for the nascent magazine.

In the meantime, Grant kept busy with other projects as well. In 1921, she was instrumental in forming, with Ruth Hale, the Lucy Stone League. With the motto "A wife should no more take her husband's name than he should hers. My name is my identity and must not be lost," the women's rights group was the first to fight for women to be allowed to keep and use legally their maiden names after marriage. In 1922, she helped form the New York Newspaper Woman's Club (now the Newswomen's Club of New York), which, according to its website, "was born out of a desire to achieve professional equality for newswomen, meritocracy in newsrooms, and to build a network through which newswomen could help each other."

JANE GRANT

In 1925, *The New Yorker* was born, providing a sophisticated and often humorous take on the social and cultural life of Manhattan. Ross was the editor in chief; Grant was responsible for growing circulation. Over time, the magazine would broaden its scope to include politics, literature, and other topics, eventually becoming required reading for the City's sophisticates, as well as for those aiming to keep up with the haut monde.

The couple divorced in 1929; Ross continued at the magazine until 1951. Grant, abandoned by many writer-friends who hoped to stay in Ross's good favor, went on to remarry, move to Litchfield, Connecticut, work as a foreign correspondent, and start a successful mail-order gardening business. She also dreamed up a way to launch the magazine into the national consciousness: in 1943, Grant proposed a "pony" edition (that was smaller in size and heavy on cartoons) to be supplied to the armed forces overseas, an idea which, according to an online exhibit created by the University of Oregon library, was initially dismissed by Ross and the publisher.

Despite their lack of support, Grant persevered, and what she called the "little *New Yorker*" turned out to be a massive success: after the war, officers and servicemen, now devoted readers, returned home and bought subscriptions; within two years of the war's end the magazine had doubled its circulation and was now being dispersed everywhere from Cheyenne to Chicago.

Although credit for *The New Yorker* is often ascribed to Harold Ross, it was Grant's initiative and tenacity that truly established the City's iconic publication.

When *The New York Times* owner Adolph S. Ochs passed away in 1935, his daughter IPHIGENE OCHS SULZBERGER (1892–1990) became a trustee of the paper along with her husband, Arthur Hays Sulzberger, who was elected publisher and president. While Ochs Sulzberger remained mostly offstage in the paper's operations, she was also the daughter, wife, mother, mother-in-law, and grandmother of five of the paper's past and current publishers—and, as family matriarch, kept smooth the good familial relationships necessary to jointly manage a business. She also adroitly hosted a nonstop parade of VIPs and dignitaries, many on whom her family's business depended—and some with whom her husband not infrequently faced ideological conflicts.

Known as an adult for her dynamic mind and playful sense of humor, Sulzberger began developing her sophisticated social skills early in life. As a girl, she'd had to memorize and deliver a speech written by her father at a well-attended event to mark the kickoff of construction on the *Times*'s new tower at 42nd Street and Broadway. She'd also received the numerous Secret Service agents who once commandeered her home prior to the arrival of President William Howard Taft for lunch. As a teenager, she was entreated to socialize with inventor of the wireless telegraph Guglielmo Marconi—a business associate of her father who was two decades her senior; they shared a single, two-strawed ice cream soda in Coney Island.

Under Sulzberger family stewardship, which has lasted more than a century, *The New York Times* became the country's most prestigious news organization; a leading source of international news, it has also captured the most Pulitzer Prizes. And while other newspaper dynasties suffered damaging public feuds (including the Bingham clan in Louisville, Kentucky, and the Scripps family of Cincinnati, Ohio), the Sulzbergers have remained united enough to see the paper through a series of colossal changes, including the sale of its historic buildings off namesake Times Square and the construction of a skyscraper. With the invention of the Internet and its attendant decline in print readership, the century-old business model of financing editorial work with sales of print advertising was nearly destroyed; in its wake, the *Times* has needed to create a new one—while still maintaining its high journalistic standards and reputation.

In her more public roles, Ochs Sulzberger was director of the Times Company from 1917 until 1973. During WWII, she spearheaded several initiatives to assist the war effort, including the creation of *Times*-printed supplements and booklets for schools. She was also a patron of many city institutions, serving as a trustee at Barnard College, her alma mater, and the Hebrew Union College–Jewish Institute of Religion. She supported both the National Urban League and Inwood House (a home for unmarried mothers). She served as president and eventually chair of the Park Association, through which she helped restore a park in the Bronx and arranged for a chess and checkers house in Central Park.

All in all, without her devotion to her family—serving as confidant to her husband and providing what her granddaughter and biographer, Susan W. Dryfoos, described as an endless supply of loving support and humor—*The New York Times* would unlikely be the same place. Said Dryfoos: she was "the glue that held us all together."

Over the quarter century that **BARBARA WALTERS** (b. 1929) worked at *20/20*, the newsmagazine show on ABC, her interviews with dignitaries, celebrities, politicians, and ordinary people alike transformed the practice of journalism, blurred the lines between news and entertainment, and—in the days before cable television, personal computers, and the Internet—fueled the epic, decades-long war between three main television news networks.

Walters got her big break when she was hired—and called the *"Today* Girl"—for NBC's *Today* show in 1964; a decade later, in 1974, she became cohost of the show. In 1976 she moved to ABC News, becoming the first woman to coanchor an evening network news program. She possesses a rare combination of intelligence, camera presence, and charm, which enable her to ask disarmingly direct questions that often lead subjects into surprising moments of self-revelation. In 1977, for example, Bing Crosby told Walters that he wouldn't speak to any child of his who'd had premarital sex. In 1988, Robin Givens admitted fearing for her safety with her husband, Mike Tyson. And, in a prison interview, the man who shot John Lennon calmly and terrifyingly revealed that he thought by killing the legendary songwriter he would "acquire his fame."

While critics contend that Walters's interest in her guests' personal lives undermines the loftier goals of journalism, that approach has, for decades, undeniably granted her one exclusive interview after another, driving the fierce rivalry between TV news networks—even rendering some editions of *The Barbara Walters Specials* (with Super Bowl–level ratings) their own historic moments in popular culture.

Moreover, landing an interview with Walters could make—or break—someone's identity in the court of public opinion. When Monica Lewinsky broke her silence about her affair with President Bill Clinton in an interview on *20/20*, more than forty-eight million people tuned in, making it the most-watched news program to have ever been aired by a single network.

⁂

While Walters augmented serious journalism with questions about celebrities' personal lives, gossip columnist **LIZ SMITH** (b. 1923) had no qualms about admitting her fascination for the personal dramas of the famous or affluent; for four decades, she has reigned in Manhattan as the Doyenne of Dish.

After ghostwriting the Cholly Knickerbocker society and gossip column in the 1950s, and working for Helen Gurley Brown at *Cosmopolitan* magazine in the 1960s, the Texas native landed her own self-titled gossip column at the

New York Daily News in 1976. Having already befriended Elizabeth Taylor and Richard Burton, she peddled juicy tidbits that made her into the modern-day equivalent of a town crier.

Not since Walter Winchell in the 1930s and 1940s did so many people pay attention to a gossip columnist. At her peak, Smith was syndicated in more than seventy-five newspapers worldwide, as much a part of Hollywood as all the celebrities she covered.

But while readers in Peoria and Paris alike certainly enjoyed keeping up with the goings-on of NYC's elites, Smith's column played a more essential role in New York City itself. For example, investment bankers could learn about potential splits or family dramas among business partners, and studio heads and sports-team managers could keep tabs on their talent's adventures and misadventures—and try to intervene before they did too much to tarnish their images.

The speed and ease of online publishing, not to mention the invention of digital photography and video, eventually led to many people trying to imitate the Doyenne of Dish. But websites like Gawker or TMZ lack Smith's credibility—cred she took with her in 2009 after the *New York Post*, then home to her column, unceremoniously fired her; she was eighty-six at the time.

When asked about the plethora of celebrity websites and blogs in the Internet age, Smith, who at 93 continues her column for the *New York Social Diary* website, *Huffington Post*, and *Chicago Tribune Syndicate*, breezily dismissed them. "I don't pay attention to any of them," she told me. "I never know whether the stories are true."

HARLEM
RENAISSANCE

As the twentieth century entered its third decade, with the Great War finally over, the economy booming, and the atmosphere replete with messages of self-invention and social advancement through consumerism, New York in the 1920s was downright exuberant.

As word about abundant opportunities in the Big Apple spread through the South, African Americans migrated north in search of a better life. Many settled in Harlem, which led to the creation of a majority black neighborhood.

The coalescing of so many blacks, not only from the American South but also from all over the United States and the Caribbean, provided what philosopher Alain LeRoy Locke recognized as black America's "first chances for group expression and self-determination." The result: a literary, artistic, and intellectual renaissance that reshaped African American cultural identity and remade the landscape of American letters.

A key figure in this cultural moment was **ZORA NEALE HURSTON** (1891–1960), who, despite being a newcomer to the City, claimed more prizes at a 1925 literary awards dinner than any other writer.

Had anyone failed to take notice of Hurston's arrival, she made an entrance to the after-party that brought the room to a halt: striding into the room, she dramatically bellowed the title of her winning play (*"Coloooooor Struuuuuck!"*) while flinging a long, richly colored scarf around her neck. Several partygoers sought her acquaintance then and there, including Annie Nathan Meyer, a founder of Barnard College who promptly offered Hurston admission to the thirty-six-year-old school as its first black student.

Hurston, who had grown up in the black enclave of Eatonville, Florida, and whose mother had died when she was only thirteen, accepted the offer. Soon she became a member of the pack of literary bohemians—including Langston Hughes, Wallace Thurman, and Richard Bruce Nugent—who hung out in a rooming house on West 136th Street and laughingly dubbed themselves the "Niggerati." Together, these cultural troubadours swapped jokes, traded ideas, and reflected on what Hurston described later as "our business of dream weaving that we call writing."

Hurston's remarkable gifts of language and outgoing personality, which biographer Valerie Boyd described as "bodacious charm," meant she embodied the very essence of the era and the City. "When I set my hat at a certain angle and saunter down Seventh Avenue, Harlem City, feeling as snooty as the lions in front of the 42nd Street Library," she wrote in her notable 1928 essay "How It Feels to Be Colored Me," the "cosmic Zora emerges. I belong to no race nor time. I am the eternal feminine with its string of beads."

In between producing plays, poems, essays, novels, and paintings, Hurston and her pack fiercely debated whether blacks should aim to achieve success using the same paradigms established by whites or whether they were free

WHEN I SET MY HAT AT A CERTAIN
ANGLE AND SAUNTER DOWN SEVENTH
AVENUE, HARLEM CITY, FEELING AS
SNOOTY AS THE LIONS IN FRONT
OF THE 42ND STREET LIBRARY, THE
COSMIC ZORA EMERGES. I BELONG
TO NO RACE NOR TIME. I AM THE
ETERNAL FEMININE WITH ITS STRING
OF BEADS.

—ZORA NEALE HURSTON, 1928

to create their own rules. Hurston, who became an anthropologist, inadvertently answered the question by using her eloquence and ethnography to lay claim to the heritage of blacks in the rural South; with her works *Mules and Men* and *Tell My Horse*, among other writings, she demonstrated to all the world the previously underacknowledged gifts of folk culture, and how they were, in fact, an inheritance bequeathed to future generations.

Just as new ideas emerged from the uproarious decade, so, too, did new sounds. The singer we know as **BILLIE HOLIDAY** (1915–1959) was a mere fifteen years old when, waiting tables at a gin mill in Harlem where her mother worked in the kitchen, she started singing for tips. The musicians and entertainers among her customers, impressed by both her voice and her unique talent for phrasing, helped her get auditions at various nightclubs. From there she gradually became part of the neighborhood's music scene, and she was eventually discovered by the record producer John Hammond, who paired her with Benny Goodman and helped her cut her first record.

Hammond was struck by Holiday's "uncanny harmonic sense and her sense of lyric content"; after jamming with her one night in the summer of 1932, the guitarist Lawrence Lucie said that he and the other musicians hadn't previously "heard anything like that, a natural *jazz* feeling." Before long, Billie, nicknamed

"Lady Day" by saxophonist Lester Young, was working with all the top musicians of the era and headlining at Café Society in the Village.

Although she wasn't a blues singer per se, Holiday's voice evoked a blues mood. (This mood was no doubt a truthful reflection of the tragedy she had seen up close, including being brought to live and work in a brothel by her mother when she was thirteen as well as her lifelong struggle with substance abuse.) Her vocal stylings and improvisation skills rendered her the preeminent jazz singer of her day, touching off one of the City's most important and lasting cultural movements.

Between the music, the jumping nightclubs, and the white intelligentsia's sudden interest in black culture, Harlem in the 1920s was the place to be. Some would say there was no one more responsible for the conviviality above 125th Street than **A'LELIA WALKER** (1885–1931), daughter of entrepreneur and philanthropist Madam C.J. Walker, the country's first black female millionaire. (In 1905 Madam Walker started a company producing African American hair products, building it into a prosperous national chain.)

With phenomenal sums of money at her disposal, love of the arts, and experience traveling the globe in the world's most elite circles, the younger Walker hosted a series of parties at her posh townhouse on 136th Street (near what is now

Malcolm X Boulevard), where champagne flowed, nightclub quartets crooned, and urbanites of all backgrounds rubbed elbows in close quarters.

The country's first black heiress, who cut a striking nearly six-foot figure and dressed extravagantly, brought together downtown poets, financiers, white socialites, and Harlem number runners—enabling blacks and whites for the first time to socialize on near-equal terms.

And they socialized up close: Walker's parties were so notoriously well attended that even invited guests were often unable to squeeze inside. Langston Hughes recounted in his autobiography an occasion when a royal personage ("a Scandinavian prince, I believe") arrived and found no way to get through the crowds into the actual party so he sent in a message to the hostess; demonstrating both her wit and her stature, Walker sent back a message that she couldn't find a way out either, but she would gladly send refreshments to his car.

Even when she wasn't hosting a party, Walker routinely opened her home for theatrical rehearsals and art exhibitions and provided rent-free accommodations for artists. This open nature, combined with her love of dramatic fashion (she was known to wear a bejeweled turban), lead Langston Hughes to anoint her nothing less than the "joy goddess of Harlem's 1920s."

A'LELIA WALKER

THE CROOKS

The towering achievements of the great metropolis are as legendary as is its dark side, which has inspired everything from the *Batman* comics to the *Godfather* trilogy to the legends of Hell-Cat Maggie and Sadie the Goat. The latter are especially savage female gangsters who appeared in Herbert Asbury's 1928 *The Gangs of New York: An Informal History of the Underworld*; note that, though they've been portrayed as factual in numerous prominent New York histories, there is no independent proof they actually existed.

But the City's cons and crimes—which arguably began with Peter Minuit's so-called purchase of Manhattan island from the Lenape, a people who did not believe land could belong to humans individually—have always been the purview of women as well as men.

After the Civil War, Prussian émigré **FREDERICKA "MARM" MANDELBAUM** (1818–1894), a savvy street peddler in Kleindeutschland (Little Germany) on the Lower East Side, became one of the City's most infamous fences after she recognized the financial opportunity in supplying a reliable outpost for vending stolen goods. By 1865, she'd moved with her family into a clapboard house at the corner of Clinton and Rivington Streets, where she set up a dry-goods store on the ground floor. Up front, she sold items like scarves, jewelry, and bolts of silk; but in the back she made business arrangements to, ahem, inexpensively obtain the merchandise.

By the end of that decade, she was mother hen to the era's most successful organized crime ring; she'd even established a crime school on Grand Street to ensure she had a reliable supply of skilled associates. Nearly six feet tall and weighing two hundred fifty pounds, Mandelbaum helped plan heists, approved deals, and paired thieves and crooks with those who could support their more ambitious undertakings. In 1869 she arranged for the safecracker "Piano" Charlie Bullard to be broken out of jail; the same year, she gave the nod for George Leonidas Leslie to pull off the biggest bank robbery in history, using the then-revolutionary technique of stealing the lock combination in advance rather than dynamiting the safe.

These exploits, and Mandelbaum's skill at nurturing the careers of younger crooks, earned her the nickname "The Queen Among Thieves" in the era's newspapers.

One protégée of Mandelbaum was the young and beautiful **SOPHIE LEVY LYONS** (1848–1924), whose family had sent her out to steal pocketbooks before the age of six. By sixteen, Lyons was a skilled femme fatale; while her parents were both serving simultaneous terms in the slammer, Mandelbaum took her under her wing and arranged for her to attend her crime school, then sent her out to ply their trade.

CURIOUSLY ENOUGH,
THE GREATEST CRIME
PROMOTER OF MODERN
TIMES WAS A NEW YORK
WOMAN, "MOTHER"
MANDELBAUM. ALAS!
I KNEW HER WELL—
TOO WELL.

—SOPHIE LEVY LYONS, 1913

After nearly four decades of robberies, cons, and swindles and several turns in the slammer, the self-described "Queen of the Underworld" spent three years in the Detroit House of Correction, where she underwent a conversion. Filled with remorse, she worked to turn others away from crime, and in 1913 she authored her memoirs, *Why Crime Does Not Pay*, in hopes that others would realize "a life of crime is a life of hard work, great risk, and, comparatively speaking, little pay."

In 1913, Sophie Lyons began writing her memoirs, to be published in a book titled *Why Crime Does Not Pay*. It was about a decade later when quick-minded **STEPHANIE ST. CLAIR** (1897–1969), who had come to New York alone from her birthplace in Guadeloupe at age thirteen, began proving Lyons' title wrong by setting up a numbers racket in Harlem, which, according to author Shirley Stewart, eventually earned her a quarter of a million dollars a year. In *The World of Stephanie St. Clair: An Entrepreneur, Race Woman and Outlaw in Early Twentieth Century Harlem*, Stewart traces how St. Clair not only became the leader of one of the top policy banks in Harlem but also a maverick gangster who stood up to some of the era's most feared white mobsters—and triumphed.

Almost immediately after arriving at Ellis Island in 1911, St. Clair traveled north to Montreal, where her mother had arranged for her to work as a domestic. Within five years, St. Clair crossed back into the U.S. and made her way to

Harlem, where she purportedly found work at a dress factory and worked for a racketeer who was running numbers in an organized illegal betting ring.

She amassed a savings of $10,000, and using that money, she launched her own operation in 1923, a remarkable feat considering the general dearth of opportunities available to blacks. According to Stewart, in the 1920s, blacks owned less than twenty percent of Harlem's businesses.

Running a successful "policy bank" required hard work, business savvy, and the ability to steward an array of parties with various interests. Bankers like St. Clair were expected to act as neighborhood guardians: loaning money, funding community projects, and exerting their authority to keep rogues in line when the police couldn't be bothered. To receive and manage money, they had to hire and run a crew on whom they could depend. And they had to pay off the police. Every week.

St. Clair did all of that, and owing to her shrewd business sensibility and authoritative demeanor—she was known for both benevolence and a fiery temper—St. Clair became known by neighborhood residents as "Queenie." According to Ron Chepesiuk's *Gangsters of Harlem: The Gritty Underworld of New York's Most Famous Neighborhood*, St. Clair eventually employed forty runners and ten controllers, plus a support staff, making her one of the largest policy bankers in Harlem.

For a few years, life was good: St. Clair's financial success allowed her to live on an expensive avenue in an area nicknamed Sugar Hill, with neighbors like Madam C.J. Walker, the beauty product tycoon, W.E.B. Du Bois, the scholar and activist, and Thurgood Marshall, an attorney and future Supreme Court justice. But all that began to change in 1928 after Caspar Holstein, Harlem's number-one numbers operator, was kidnapped and a ransom of $50,000 paid by his associates on a Friday night.

Astute white mobsters—who had previously ignored Harlem—noticed this sum was produced in cash after banks had closed, tipping them off to just how much money flowed above 110th Street. The notorious bootlegger Dutch Schultz began a violent takeover of Harlem operations and quickly succeeded in putting most of St. Clair's colleagues out of business.

Rather than go into hiding, St. Clair, who had been dutifully paying protection money to the cops in her local precinct for years, declared war. She purchased a series of advertisements in the popular *Amsterdam News* decrying the violence perpetuated on black residents, detailing Schultz's harassment and outing the widespread corruption in law enforcement. These efforts drew St. Clair into politics and led to a crackdown on police corruption—and further inflamed Schultz. Meanwhile, as other numbers-runners backed down, ceding their businesses or watching them become violently seized, St. Clair held firm, demanding of her male employees, "You are men and you will desert me now? What kind of men would desert a lady in a fight?"

Even after Schultz put out a contract on her life, St. Clair refused to be intimidated, Stewart reports: In 1932, she walked into a storefront business controlled by Schultz's operation, smashed their plate glass display cases, and demanded they and their cronies leave Harlem. St. Clair was finally relieved of Schultz's interference when a gangster murdered him in 1935.

Three years later, St. Clair orchestrated her own demise when she pulled the trigger of a gun three times, firing shots at a lover, landing her in a Westchester prison.

Criminality takes all kinds of forms. Later in the twentieth century, Cheng Chui Ping, known as **SISTER PING** (1949–2014), became what the FBI called "one of the most powerful underworld figures in New York." Over at least two decades, she smuggled thousands of Chinese into the United States.

Working out of a variety store in Chinatown, Sister Ping set up an illegal banking network through which aspiring immigrants from China, especially those from her native Fujian province, could wire her tens of thousands of dollars. She smuggled in people on ships. While legions of grateful illegals said she provided them with a new life, prosecutors proved that she had put many desperate charges on faulty ships, leading to an untold number of drownings. Plus, in instances when safe arrivals couldn't afford to pay, Ping sent members of the notoriously violent Fuk Ching gang to abduct, beat, torture, or rape them until relatives made good on their debts.

In 1993, the toll of human smuggling became highly visible when a rusty freighter called the *Golden Venture* ran aground in the Rockaways loaded with three hundred starving Fujianese refugees. Ten of them died, including one of Sister Ping's customers. Though Ping fled, she was eventually tracked down and arrested in Hong Kong in 2000, after which she was tried in federal court in

Manhattan. Aided by the testimony of witnesses from around the world—including from Guatemala, Canada, the United States, and Hong Kong—she was convicted of conspiracy to smuggle aliens and take hostages, money laundering, and trafficking in ransom proceeds. In 2014, at the age of sixty-five, the woman known by her associates as the "Mother of all Snakeheads" died in a Texas prison, just eight years after receiving a thirty-five-year sentence.

While Ping was being tried in one federal courtroom in New York, another woman, the left-wing attorney **LYNNE STEWART** (b. 1939) was being tried and convicted in another.

Over a decades-long career that was much admired by left-leaning colleagues, Stewart, a former librarian, represented battered women, poor blacks, and Latinos accused of petty crimes. Over the years, she took on increasingly more high-profile cases, like a former member of the Weather Underground and a black man accused of shooting six NYPD cops.

But it was during her representation of Sheik Omar Abdel-Rahman, the blind Sheik who was convicted in a 1990s plot to blow up New York landmarks (including the 1993 bombing of the World Trade Center), that her conduct crossed the boundary into unlawfulness.

The Sheik, seen as a spiritual leader of the worldwide jihad movement and an opponent of the Hosni Mubarak regime in Egypt, was so dangerous that federal authorities ordered Stewart to sign an agreement that she would not relay any messages from him to the outside world, as his followers would receive them as official directives. In violation of the order, she held a press conference in 2000 where she related that the Sheik rescinded his support for a cease fire by the Islamic Group, a statement she later described as "an advisory." On September 11, 2001, terrorists succeeded in carrying out a major attack inside the United States, something Abdel-Rahman called for in his 1998 fatwa.

Stewart was sentenced to twenty-eight months in prison; it was later increased to ten years after she showed a lack of remorse, including telling reporters that she "would do it again."

She went to prison in 2009. In 2013, she was diagnosed with terminal breast cancer, then granted "compassionate release." She returned to Brooklyn in early 2014 to live with her son and now posts messages on a website where, as of early 2016, she refers collectively to herself and like-minded readers as "anarchists."

THE AUTHORITIES

It wasn't until 1844 that the state legislature decided to replace the City's old system of policing—which consisted primarily of eighty night watchmen. In 1845, a "Day and Night Police" law was established, calling for a company of 800 men to work separate day and night shifts. It would take another nine years before training was implemented and full uniforms adopted, which included a leather helmet and a twenty-two inch baton (to be used only for "urgent self-defense").

Over the next half century, rival political factions would tussle for control of the force—and the myriad of benefits from its widespread corruption—but around the turn of the century, reformers like Charles Parkhurst and police commissioner Theodore Roosevelt helped set the force on a path of professionalization.

Although women had served as police "matrons" since 1882—they conducted searches on female prisoners and kept watch over juveniles—it wasn't until 1915 that a police captain began urging his superiors to hire women for the pickpocket squad—a practice already utilized by law enforcement organizations overseas.

It took twenty years of convincing, but finally, in 1935, four women were assigned to the pickpocket squad on a provisional basis, including Irish-born **MARY SHANLEY** (1896–1989) who was five foot eight and weighed 160 pounds.

On her first day on the job, Shanley and a colleague nabbed a suspect they saw stealthily opening and closing customers' pocketbooks on a department store counter. Two years later, Shanley landed on the second page of *The New York Times* after recognizing two known criminals in a subway station; she had chased them uptown and across Times Square, then overtook one while twice firing her revolver in the air to halt the other.

In 1938, Dead-Shot Mary (as she had come to be known) impressed colleagues by chasing notorious "hook" Chinatown Charlie down Fifth Avenue, then overtaking him and putting him under arrest. While she wasn't shy about pulling out her gun, she also earned admiration from her superiors for her ability to halt criminals using nothing more than her booming, Irish-brogued voice. Case in point: at a Macy's store in Queens, she ended a tense, ten-minute standoff with a pistol-waving twenty-two-year-old threatening to kill customers. How? By quietly approaching him from behind, then snapping: "Drop that gun, boy!"

Though Mary Shanley and her colleagues paved the way for the next class of female officers, no one would think the police department ever lacked for sexism. In 1940, when the police academy graduated its first full class of policewomen—there were eight, including thirty-one-year-old Bronx-born

MARY SHANLEY, "DEAD-SHOT MARY"

146

GERTRUDE "GERTIE" SCHIMMEL (1918–2015)—the new officers were issued black pocketbooks (with space to hold their pistols), and the mayor welcomed them with an admonishment to "try to keep that girlish figure."

Twenty-one years later, when a fellow policewoman, Felicia Shpritzer, prepared a lawsuit against the City for not letting her take the test for promotion to sergeant, Schimmel helped her out.

Despite the police commissioner's arguments that women were physically unable to handle advanced jobs, the court ruled in Shpritzer's favor. Both Schimmel and Shpritzer took the exam; after earning the two highest scores, both were promoted in 1965—although they were only allowed to supervise women. (A front-page story in the next day's *New York Times* was careful to reassure the public that "no policeman will be supervised by a woman.")

Six years after that, in 1971, Schimmel, who frequently worked the night shift so she could be home to see her sons off to school in the morning, became the NYPD's first female captain. In 1978, she was named the first female deputy chief.

During her tenure, Schimmel, whose blunt, voluble, and occasionally profane conversation style led Anna Quindlen to later describe her as "the Ethel Merman of the Police Department," helped lay the groundwork for women to finally go on street patrols and in radio cars.

Despite these advances, many NYC groups remained resistant to change—including some policemen's wives, who argued that women weren't up to the task of providing backup to their husbands. But Schimmel adroitly dismissed their concerns. "Nothing is factual, it's all emotional," she told a newspaper in 1974. "The men make allowances for each other. They won't tell you about the men they don't want to work with."

While Schimmel was climbing the ranks at the NYPD, a young graduate of University of Virginia School of Law named **LINDA FAIRSTEIN** (b. 1947) went to work for the New York County District Attorney's office. In 1976, she was appointed chief of a sex crimes unit that had been founded just two years earlier by Richard H. Kuh, the Interim Manhattan District Attorney preceding Robert Morgenthau, and Assistant District Attorney Leslie Crocker Snyder.

After prosecuting her first few cases, Fairstein, who had grown up near the Bronx in Westchester County and attended Vassar College, was appalled to see judges' cavalier attitude toward sentencing rapists—as they just returned to the streets to assault more women. And so, over what would become more than a quarter century of running the sex crimes unit, Fairstein developed a number of innovations toward holding perpetrators of sex crimes as accountable as other violent criminals, all with a mind to keep them off the streets.

This process included changing what had been standard procedure: handing cases off to different officers. Recognizing that victims of assault often found it difficult to share their stories, Fairstein ensured victims continued to work with the same person; this didn't just help them feel more comfortable—it also made it more likely they'd ultimately testify in court. She also started a program to teach counselors in City hospitals how to help victims report crimes. She convinced the NYPD to include prosecutors in rape investigations from their beginnings. And, following a successful approach devised by a prosecutor in Wisconsin, Fairstein became one of the first lawyers in the nation to indict DNA profiles of yet-to-be-identified rapists in order to prevent statutes of limitations from hindering eventual prosecution.

Fairstein's work on two high-profile cases in the eighties, "The Preppy Murder" of eighteen-year-old Jennifer Levin in 1986 and the "Central Park jogger" case in 1989 (which was prosecuted by Elizabeth Lederer, who worked in Fairstein's unit), put her name in the public spotlight—as did a side career writing popular crime novels.

But Fairstein's most lasting contribution to New York City was her relentless willingness to prosecute commonplace date or acquaintance rape, which had been all but ignored by law enforcement for centuries. New York's district attorneys rarely brought charges against rapists who were known to the victims (at least in part) because, until 1975, state law required a corroborating witness; as that's hard to come by when attacks occur in intimate settings, it made it all but impossible for prosecutors to procure indictments. (In 1969, for example, there were more than one thousand arrests for rape in New York City, but only eighteen convictions.) "When I got out of college in 1969, an all-women's college, I don't think I'd heard the word 'rape' four times in my four years there," she told me. "It was something that people didn't talk about. They were worried about public safety, but rape was not accepted as criminal conduct, nor did the media pay any attention to it."

By taking on such cases, as well as those where a victim drank alcohol or took drugs or initially consented, Fairstein helped legitimize the idea that women should have ultimate control over their own bodies. Her work and stance also began shifting public opinion—and, by extension, jurors' decisions—away from the long-entrenched habit of blaming the victim.

As she succeeded in prosecutions, even winning several instances of rape by a spouse, New York's sex crime unit became a model for prosecutors across the country. Adding to her influence, in 1993 Fairstein published *Sexual Violence: Our War Against Rape*, which became a handbook of sorts for law enforcement officers and activists nationwide. In 1999, she began work on helping the City overcome its backlog of more than sixteen thousand unexamined rape kits; this effort, which took four years to complete, cemented the reputation of New York law enforcement as being well ahead of its counterparts in other cities.

While the threat of rape will never fully disappear, thanks to Linda Fairstein, the City felt safer—to residents, to college students, and to those students' parents.

⁂

In 1993, a no-nonsense lawyer named **MARY JO WHITE** (b. 1947) was confirmed as the United States Attorney for the Southern District of New York, a prestigious federal law enforcement body that predates the Department of Justice in Washington by more than eighty years.

White moved into her office in 1993, just three months after the first terrorist attack on the World Trade Center, in which a bomb in a parking garage underneath the north tower killed six people. Over the next nine years the SDNY corps, led by White—who decorated her office with Yankees memorabilia and sometimes rode a motorcycle to work—prosecuted a steady stream of white-collar criminals, civil rights violators, leaders of international drug cartels, and public corruption cases.

But while all that was taking place, she was also quietly working with the Joint Terrorism Task Force (JTTF), a group of detectives from the NYPD and FBI who collaborated on monitoring local and international threats.

Facing a new kind of enemy—individual terrorists, rather than a state that declared war—White devised new ways to fight them in the court of law; these innovations were necessary because previous enemies of the state had been thwarted only militarily. In 1993, she secured an indictment against Sheik Omar Abdel-Rahman, a blind Egyptian cleric, for his role in plotting to blow up the United Nations and other NYC landmarks; she charged him under a Civil War–era seditious conspiracy law, which makes it illegal to plan to wage war against the government.

In 1996, White indicted Khalid Sheikh Mohammed—later the mastermind of the 9/11 attacks—for his role in the foiled plot to blow up nearly a dozen American jetliners as they flew over the Pacific Ocean. Two years later, she obtained an indictment against Osama bin Laden for conspiring to destroy U.S. defense installations and for the bombings of U.S. embassies in East Africa. Afterward, White's SDNY helped to convict an Algerian man tied to a plot to blow up the Los Angeles International Airport during the 2000 millennial celebration.

By 2001, there was no prosecutor in the country with more expertise in investigating and successfully prosecuting international terrorism. Having been appointed by President Bill Clinton, she was ready to resign when President George W. Bush took office in 2001. But she stayed on to oversee a number of high-profile terrorism and political-corruption matters for another year, departing in 2002.

After more than a decade in private practice at Debevoise & Plimpton, White returned to the public sector in 2013, becoming the chair of the Securities and Exchange Commission. There, as the federal government's top financial cop, she brought a historic number of enforcement cases against companies and individuals, and worked to get stricter standards for advisors who counsel average investors on stock, bond, and fund purchases.

Unlike some of her predecessors and successors, White never sought the spotlight; quite the contrary: she took pains to stay out of it. Beloved by her staff, she possessed an interesting combination of no-nonsense attitude toward work and mischievous sense of humor, as she often participated in office pranks. Before she became the first and only woman to lead SDNY, she earned a place in NYC prosecutors' lore when, after a male colleague challenged her to a tennis match, she drove her red Honda motorcycle onto the court with the song "I Am Woman" blaring from a tape player mounted to the back.

Measuring a full foot shorter than her opponent's height of six feet, she won.

THE
GREAT WHITE WAY

ETHEL WATERS (1896–1977), the daughter of a young girl who had been raped at knifepoint by a family acquaintance, grew up in poverty and neglect. Yet her treacherous beginnings didn't stop her from leaving a lasting mark. The cusp of the Roaring Twenties found Waters in Harlem, singing in Edmond's Cellar; by the time she arrived on Broadway in the all-black revue *Africana* in 1927, she was already a star on the pop charts and in the black theater, having channeled the emotional violence of her childhood into a soul-tugging voice that transformed jazz into the blues and created pop hits like "Dinah" and "Sweet Georgia Brown."

But it was her rendition of the torch song "Stormy Weather" at the Cotton Club in 1933 that moved composer and songwriter Irving Berlin to immediately cast her in a new musical revue he was writing with Moss Hart: *As Thousands Cheer.* When Waters took the stage of the Music Box Theatre five months later, she joined the then-nascent ranks of black women who'd appeared on Broadway with a white cast. In his rich biography *Heat Wave: The Life and Career of Ethel Waters,* historian Donald Bogle documents how whites previously excluded even the most talented black performers, giving rise to the joke that the Great White Way—the nickname for the stretch of Broadway between 42nd and

53rd Streets—was named not for its blinding marquee lights but for its intention of remaining lily-white.

In *As Thousands Cheer*, Waters mesmerized audiences night after night. And she performed despite tremendous personal costs; not only did she endure hostile treatment from white cast members, she nightly had to revisit the darkest emotional depths in order to perform "Supper Time," a song about a woman's response to learning her husband has been lynched—a number so moving it routinely stopped the show. Still, her talent and discipline did not go unrewarded; during the run of *As Thousands Cheer*, Waters was believed to be the highest-paid female actor on Broadway.

Six years before Billie Holiday recorded "Strange Fruit"—the haunting song that shone a light on the horror of lynching—Waters introduced contemporary social commentary to the Great White Way, marking an important shift in both the New York entertainment scene and American popular culture. While it is true that it was Berlin who'd conceived of this new direction for musical theater, he understood that only someone with Waters's theatrical and vocal capacities could actually pull it off.

Waters would later star in a popular NBC radio program; become the first black woman to have her own network TV sitcom, *Beulah*; and ultimately tour with the evangelist Billy Graham. But it was her performance on Broadway that is most significant, as it began the transition from the glittery, sugary-sweet content of the follies to revues that contained satire as well as frank, honest portrayals about life in all its beauty and harshness.

WHAT I'D ALSO DISCOVERED
WHILE I HAD MY BACK TO
THE WALL WAS THAT HUMAN
KINDNESS WAS DEPTHLESS,
IMMEASURABLE, AND BROKE
ACROSS ALL COLOR LINES
AND GEOGRAPHICAL
BOUNDARIES.

—ETHEL WATERS, 1950

To be sure, comedy was big business, and **ETHEL MERMAN** (1908–1984) was Broadway's comedy queen. Between 1930 and 1959 she created more than a dozen roles, including the leads in some of musical theater's most iconic shows—*Anything Goes* (1934), *Annie Get Your Gun* (1946), and *Gypsy* (1959)—helping to create what was known as musical theater's Golden Age and solidifying New York as its epicenter.

Merman, née Ethel Zimmerman, was born in her grandmother's house in Astoria, Queens. Growing up, she often went to vaudeville shows at the Palace Theatre in Manhattan, where she saw stars like Sophie Tucker and Fanny Brice. (We'll meet Fanny Brice again in the "Wisecrackers" chapter.) Though she never took music lessons, she sang for WWI soldiers as a child; after finishing high school, she moonlighted as a nightclub singer while working as a secretary for the B-K Booster Vacuum Brake Company. Then in 1930, while singing between film shorts at Brooklyn's Paramount Theatre, a Broadway producer caught her act and immediately brought her to meet George and Ira Gershwin.

Soon after, Merman debuted in their musical *Girl Crazy*, where her powerful, take-charge voice electrified the room. "Here was a star who could sell a song all the way up to the second balcony, and win laughs to boot," said theater historian John Kenrick, noting how, at the time, theaters did not have sound designers.

Though Merman appeared in numerous movies, her brassy style and non-dainty looks hampered her having a broader film career, especially as male-run Hollywood preferred to cast more stereotypically feminine leading ladies. But her bold sound, combined with crystal-clear diction and precise pitch, made her an ideal muse for songwriters like the Gershwins, Irving Berlin, and Cole Porter.

After playing the eighth (and last) Dolly Levi in *Hello, Dolly!* in 1970—a show written with her in mind that she'd nonetheless turned down about a decade earlier—Merman retired from the Broadway stage, having indelibly altered New York's theater scene. She continued to make TV appearances, including one on *The Muppet Show*, where she memorably reprised "There's No Business Like Show Business."

In 1939, the same year that Ethel Waters was becoming the first black singer to appear on television and Ethel Merman appeared in a frisky but ultimately unpopular show called *Du Barry Was a Lady*, a New York University drama student named **BETTY COMDEN** (1917–2006)—a graduate from Brooklyn's famed Erasmus Hall High School—joined with Adolph Green and several friends to launch a cabaret act at the Village Vanguard.

The group got a boost when a young musician friend of Green's dropped in to accompany them on the piano. Several years later that musician, Leonard Bernstein, collaborating with the choreographer Jerome Robbins, asked Comden and Green to write the libretto and lyrics to go with their

NEW YORK, NEW YORK,

A HELLUVA TOWN.

THE BRONX IS UP,

BUT THE BATTERY'S DOWN.

THE PEOPLE RIDE IN

A HOLE IN THE GROUN'.

NEW YORK, NEW YORK,

IT'S A HELLUVA TOWN.

—FROM "NEW YORK, NEW YORK," BY
BETTY COMDEN AND ADOLPH GREEN
FROM THE 1944 MUSICAL *ON THE TOWN*

show. The resulting musical, *On the Town*, opened on Broadway in 1944; featuring the story of three sailors on shore leave in Manhattan, it was an instant smash.

The Hollywood studio Metro-Goldwyn-Mayer quickly adapted *On The Town* for film (although the word "helluva" in its opening song was changed to "wonderful" in keeping with industry standards), and the show inaugurated a remarkable sixty-year writing partnership through which Comden and Green would give the Great White Way musicals like *Billion Dollar Baby*, *Wonderful Town*, *Applause*, and *The Will Rogers Follies*.

Their contributions to Hollywood's Golden Age were likewise significant and included screenplays for *Auntie Mame* and *Singin' in the Rain*; the latter, which the American Film Institute considered the greatest movie musical of all time, fueled the dissemination of ideas from New York stages to screens nationwide.

Over the years Comden and Green collected seven Tony Awards, and in 1980 Betty was named to the Songwriters Hall of Fame. And yet, despite her writing successes, Comden always considered herself a performer foremost; for example, in 1958 she and Green put on a two-person off-Broadway show, which earned an Obie Award. All the same, her legacy as one of the most important librettists in the history of American musical comedy is unmatched—a legacy that's especially remarkable given the dearth of female writers during this era.

THE EDITRIXES

Manhattan's garment district, which began as a manufacturing center for prêt-à-porter (ready-to-wear clothing) in the 1850s, still anchors a broad array of designers, showrooms, and wholesalers off Seventh Avenue. But the heart of New York's identity as a fashion capital today is Fashion Week, an annual affair devised in the 1940s by fashion empress **ELEANOR LAMBERT** (1903–2003), which she originally called "Press Week."

Lambert came to New York via art school in Indiana. Having always been interested in fashion as an art form, in 1939, she became the director of the New York Dress Institute, the industry's first promotional organization. There she convinced oft-competitive individual designers to group their shows to create a large showcase for the City's talent. This enabled saturated media coverage, from both local and overseas reporters, which, in turn, established New York as a place where designers could make their mark—or fail to impress.

In 1962 Lambert founded the Council of Fashion Designers of America, which she also ran for decades thereafter. She relentlessly championed the City's designers in the face of Euro-centricity among the haut monde, and she was instrumental in getting American fashion editors to finally pay attention to stateside work. A big turning point came in 1973: at a fashion show she organized at the Palace of Versailles, New York designers outshone their French counterparts, making the event what was widely considered to be a defining moment in the acceptance of American fashion.

Lambert, whose father and grandfather produced circus shows, had a particular knack for interesting the public, which derived from her appreciation of spectacle and fun. And so she introduced the practice of holding over-the-top fashion shows for charity and entertainment; she also produced events at the 1964 New York World's Fair, as well as several Radio City Music Hall Easter spectaculars. She was an early supporter of the Metropolitan Museum of Art's Costume Institute Benefit, and she helped conceive its first gala benefit in 1948, dubbing it the "Party of the Year"—a title that has so far lasted nearly seven decades.

Lambert promoted the cause of New York's designers throughout her life. She even continued—almost up until her death at one hundred—to host an exclusive Fashion Week–kickoff tradition: an annual luncheon at her Fifth Avenue apartment held for out-of-town fashion reporters and City friends.

⁂

Two fashion designers were particularly instrumental in establishing New York as the global headquarters for the fashion industry. One was Diane von Fürstenberg, who in 1970 opened a Seventh Avenue showroom, from which she soon introduced her wrap dress design. And Anna Sui, who began her atelier in her Chelsea apartment in the 1980s and, in time, would see her designs strut into boutiques around the world.

But if the essence of fashion is self-expression, perhaps no individual was more responsible for inspiring and empowering the City's trendsetters than a self-described downtown "delinquent" named **PATRICIA FIELD** (b. 1941) who, since the early 1990s, has dyed her hair the color of red hots.

Field spent her early childhood in Manhattan surrounded by clothing: her Turkish Armenian father and Greek mother were partners in a dry cleaning store on Third Avenue and 74th Street, two blocks away from where she attended school on 76th. "I would start my day at my parents' store, have a coffee and a roll, and then go to school," she told me.

During high school, she'd travel from her home in Queens (where they moved when she was eight) to the Village to spend time at jazz clubs and nightclubs, for which she and her friends would dress up. Harnessing her delight in dressing up, in 1966, at the age of twenty-four, she opened a clothing store—Pants Pub—with a friend in Greenwich Village on New York University's campus. In 1971 the store had a new name and location—Patricia Field, on 8th Street—which offered a wild, daring array of clothes concisely described by one observer as a "punk rock orgy of shreds, leather, pleather, feathers, and frills." Dazzling stretch lamé mini dresses and Day-Glo corsets intermingled with slashed riding pants and cropped leather jackets.

Indeed, punk priestesses like Debbie Harry and Patti Smith shopped there in the 1970s. But with Field's enjoyment of the theatrics of gay theater and burlesque, plus the store's proximity to Christopher Street in the West Village—a central hub for the NYC gay life—it also became a trusted supplier for the City's transvestites and drag queens, who especially appreciated Field's embrace of body-celebrating vestments.

"I love legs, I love the body. I love energy," Field once told an interviewer.

The store also became a daytime clubhouse for young people with amazing creative talents who had difficulty fitting in elsewhere. "I gave the [transvestites] and the gay kids jobs because they were visually interesting," Field told me. "The way they put themselves together, they were stylists of their own kind, and they exuded fashion. I never looked at them as 'you're gay,' 'you're straight,' 'you're underage,' whatever. It was totally creative and visual."

Not only could a transvestite count on "House of Field" having white patent leather go-go boots in size 13W, but as the 1980s club scene took hold, and the store mimicked—and helped fuel—the energy of the downtown club scene, it also came to be a secret among designers; John Galliano, Domenico Dolce and Stefano Gabbana, and other fashion insiders turned to Field for inspiration or just the right outfit-completing accent. She also had an eye for artistic talent and put on shows for street artists like Keith Haring and Jean-Michel Basquiat before they were embraced by the art community. "They were part of our crowd," Field nonchalantly explained.

So visionary was Field's style that, in 1987, the director Michael Mann asked her to work as a stylist for the short-lived TV series *Crime Story*. A few years later, she designed costumes for a film, *Miami Rhapsody*, starring Mia Farrow and Sarah Jessica Parker, who later recommended Field to Darren Star, creator of the HBO series *Sex and the City,* for which she produced such statement, of-the-moment outfits that the show became as much a showcase for New York fashion as for the adventures of its characters.

That success led to a second career for Field, who for the last three decades has been designing costumes for TV shows and films including *The Devil Wears Prada,* for which she received an Oscar nomination.

After being evicted by her alma mater from her 8th Street store and home (for twenty-one years she lived in an apartment above the boutique), she relocated the store, first to West Broadway in SoHo, then in 2005 to the Bowery. But in 2015 she closed its doors for good, freeing herself to tackle new projects, like launching a line of artist-painted clothing and dressing performers for an Italian operatic lingerie show on ice. Today, in her seventies and still fond of fishnets and Lycra dresses, Field remains the epitome of New York chic.

THE ARTISTS

Although a significant craft movement began taking shape in rural America after the industrial revolution, artists looking to push the boundaries of traditional portraiture and landscapes flocked to New York, and many of them created work that would permanently alter the cityscape.

HILDRETH MEIÈRE (1892–1961), a daughter of New York gentry, became a muralist after cultivating her drawing and painting skills in Florence, Italy, and working with a naval map maker at the Brooklyn Navy Yard during World War I. In 1928 she received commissions to design interior mosaics in Manhattan's Temple Emanu-El and St. Bartholomew's Episcopal Church. Afterward she worked on many architectural projects, both in New York and in other states. But it was an opportunity in 1931 to design the lobby at One Wall Street, located at the corner of Wall and Broadway, that lead to her creating what future critics would regard as an Art Deco masterpiece.

"The Red Room" features nearly nine thousand square feet of red and gold glass tile mosaic with geometric patterns that stretch up to the three-story vaulted ceiling. The use of linear patterns, combined with the ceiling shape and saturated color, causes the room to glow a brilliant orange toward the top, creating one of the City's most stunning spaces.

Meière's career continued for decades; she served as director of the Municipal Art Society of New York and was eventually the first woman appointed to the NYC Art Commission. But it is her Art Deco designs that remain a defining feature of the cityscape, most notably on the south facade of Radio City Music Hall, where the triptych of medallions she designed in 1932 still visually define the Rockefeller Center complex.

BERENICE ABBOTT (1898–1991), whose penetrating saucer-shaped eyes hinted at her perceptivity, discovered photography while working in Paris as a darkroom assistant to the Dadaist Man Ray. Thereafter she set up a studio where she snapped portraits of many of the era's leading lights.

When she returned to New York in 1929, struck by the rapid modernization taking place all around her, she conceived of what would become *Changing New York*, her now-iconic collection of black-and-white photos taken over a ten-year period that encapsulates both the historic and ever-changing nature of NYC.

During the first few years of the project, she staved off poverty by shooting portraits and teaching photography classes at the New School for Social Research. In 1935 she was hired by the Federal Art Project (FAP), a Depression-era government program related to the Works Project Administration, receiving a monthly salary of $145 plus assistants, a secretary, and a 1930 Ford Roadster.

Abbott's near-mathematical compositions simultaneously capture the

DOES NOT THE VERY
WORD "CREATIVE" MEAN
TO BUILD, TO INITIATE,
TO GIVE OUT, TO ACT—
RATHER THAN TO BE ACTED
UPON, TO BE SUBJECTIVE?

—BERENICE ABBOTT, 1989

physical body of the City's architecture while using light and human elements to pay tribute to its expansion into a booming modern metropolis.

When her FAP funding ran out, Abbott authored a highly respected guide to photography, invented various types of photographic equipment, and became a pioneering science photographer. But the jewel of her legacy remains the 1939 publication of *Changing New York*, a landmark in documentary photography containing images that dazzle to this day.

It wasn't until the 1940s that critics began taking note of sculptures by Ukraine-born **LOUISE NEVELSON** (1899–1988), a collagist of sorts who worked in wood, clay, and found objects. But even once noticed, her work was nonetheless often dismissed on account of her gender: after her first solo show in 1941, a critic wrote, "We learned the artist is a woman, in time to check our enthusiasm . . . otherwise we might have hailed these sculptural expressions as by surely a great figure among moderns."

In the 1950s, Nevelson's work evolved into large-scale walls. She hit her stride working with irregularly shaped wood that she painted a uniform color. Eventually, critics could no longer deny her bravado, and she finally earned widespread recognition; in 1959, she was featured in MoMA's landmark exhibition *Sixteen Americans*.

Two decades later, in 1979, she made her most visible imprint on New York by designing a set of sculptures in Cor-Ten steel that appear to float like flags above a triangular plaza in the financial district. On September 14, 1978, a decade before her death, Mayor Ed Koch proclaimed the site, where Maiden Lane intersects with Liberty and William Streets, the Louise Nevelson Plaza, the first public plaza in New York City to be named after an artist.

⁂

In 1938, French artist **LOUISE BOURGEOIS** (1911–2010) moved to New York where she, like Nevelson, studied at the Art Students League of New York. By the late 1940s and 1950s, her work appeared in solo shows in various New York galleries.

Her dark, sexually explicit subjects were rare for female artists in this era; later in life she revealed that her work was an effort to overcome the childhood trauma of learning about her father's sexual infidelities with a governess who lived with her family.

Throughout the sixties, Bourgeois experimented with new materials, like latex, plaster, and rubber. With these she created hanging sculptures, like the provocative and biomorphic *Fillette* (1968), a dismembered yet erect penis that simultaneously references castration and a distorted female figure.

In the 1970s she became a voice for anti-censorship. She also began shaping the next generation of artists by teaching at Pratt Institute, Brooklyn College, and The Cooper Union, as well as by holding weekly salons at her home in Chelsea, where she'd critique younger artists. (Her frank manner and dry sense of humor led students to name the gatherings "Sunday, bloody Sundays.")

In 1982, when Bourgeois was seventy-one, she had her first retrospective at MoMA—only the second ever given to a female artist by that institution (the first was for Georgia O'Keeffe in 1946). She continued to work obsessively well into her nineties, playing with new shapes, like giant spiders, to explore themes of fear, anxiety, and sexual victimization. She died in 2010 at the age of ninety-eight.

From a very young age, Tokyo-born **YOKO ONO** (b. 1933) showed an interest in music and creative exploration. She first studied classical musical training at one of Japan's most prestigious private schools, Gakushuin University, where she was also the first female student to enroll in the philosophy department. Then, in the early 1950s, after moving with her family to suburban Westchester, she enrolled in Sarah Lawrence College, where she continued her studies and published a play in the school's literary magazine.

Drawn to the work of experimental composers, she began spending time with other artists in downtown Manhattan. In 1960, she rented a loft where she and composer La Monte Young organized a series of music and performance-art events. These events, which drew visionary thinkers like John Cage and Marcel

Duchamp, proved pivotal in the formation of New York's avant-garde art scene. Participants included electronic music composer Richard Maxfield; Simone Forti, a post-modern dancer and choreographer; and Jackson Mac Low, a multimedia performance artist and poet. The series became legendary.

Ono also presented her own conceptual pieces, like "Painting to Be Stepped On," a canvas on which the audience was invited to walk. In July 1961, she mounted her first show, *Paintings and Drawings*, at a gallery established by George Maciunas, a prominent member of Fluxus, a loose group of artists inspired to challenge common perceptions of the role of art.

Later creations included "Cut Piece," in which Ono invited the audience to use scissors to cut of parts of the clothing she wore while she remained seated, unmoving. The effect was potent and, for some, traumatic, as it revealed the ways in which sexual violence is perpetrated on women. Other performance works consisted of engaging participants in various acts, such as lighting a match and watching it burn out; in 1964, she published a collection of short writings tied to the conceptual performance series in the celebrated book *Grapefruit*.

While in London in 1966 to attend the Destruction in Art Symposium, she met the musician John Lennon. Ono and Lennon began collaborating on films and recordings, and sharing a mutual interest in promoting peace, they organized two weeklong "bed-ins," inviting the press and members of the public into their hotel bedroom to discuss it. They also commissioned billboards in New York and other cities that proclaimed WAR IS OVER! IF YOU WANT IT.

Deeply interested in music, she formed the Plastic Ono Band in 1968, which created rock-inspired compositions for which she provided ululating vocals and other primal sounds. Band members would include Lennon and Ono, Eric Clapton, and Billy Preston. Ono and Lennon continued working as a duo as well, creating six albums, including *Some Time in New York City* (1972). Meanwhile, she ran newspaper ads for an unsanctioned, one-woman show at The Museum of Modern Art; visitors were left to ponder their conceptions of the meaning of a show after encountering a sign on which Ono invited them to track flies she claimed to have released on the museum grounds.

After enduring Lennon's murder in 1980, Ono continued to record music, including a collaboration with her son Sean Lennon, and wrote an Off-Broadway musical, *New York Rock*.

While Lennon's fame as a member of the Beatles caused some fans to dismiss her as a sycophant, several retrospectives of her work at major museums throughout the world made clear the prescient nature of her ideas, and the extent to which they predated her relationship with Lennon.

Meanwhile, Ono's public activism for non-violence and world peace has continued steadily: in 2012, she and her son Sean enlisted 150 artists to join them in Artists Against Fracking (posting a large billboard on the Major Deegan Expressway that read: GOVERNOR CUOMO: IMAGINE THERE'S NO FRACKING.).

And every year in spring, the tranquil, living memorial she created for Lennon in Central Park, named Strawberry Fields, blooms anew and demonstrates her enduring message of choosing to respond to aggression and pain with harmony.

SOUNDTRACK TO THE CITY

When **ELLA FITZGERALD** (1917–1996), a seventeen-year-old from Yonkers, put her name in the lottery to perform during Amateur Night at the Apollo Theater in 1934, she had been planning to dance. But when she was called to the stage immediately after the Edwards Sisters, an impressive tap dance duo, she feared she wouldn't measure up and chose to sing instead.

It was a fortuitous decision: as she crooned "Judy," a favorite song of her mother's written by Hoagy Carmichael, her resonant tones and rich, melodious interpretations brought down the house. The audience demanded encore after encore. And Benny Carter, a professional saxophonist and arranger in the house band that night, resolved to introduce Fitzgerald to contacts who could help launch her career, as did Bardu Ali, a musician who immediately brought her to meet Chick Webb.

Fitzgerald had been orphaned at fifteen when her mother died in a car accident in the Great Depression, struggling alone for two years. But in a matter of months after her Apollo break, she was fronting the Chick Webb Orchestra. Within two years she was performing at the Savoy Ballroom and had recorded her first song. And in 1938, four years after her Apollo debut, she released "A-Tisket A-Tasket," a catchy adult version of a child's rhyme; it sold one million copies, making her a star.

As the era of big band swing moved into bebop, a term the jazz historian Barry Ulanov traced to one of Fitzgerald's spontaneous riffs, she became the master of scat. And, frequently collaborating with all of the era's other hottest jazz performers—like Duke Ellington, Benny Goodman, and Dizzy Gillespie —she set New York's music clubs on fire.

In the 1940s and 1950s, her definitive recordings of the work of America's leading songwriters helped canonize the Great American Songbook; in time, "The First Lady of Song" became one of the most popular jazz singers in the world.

During her lifetime she sold over forty million albums and won thirteen Grammy awards. Her wide-ranging, pitch-perfect voice and incomparable artistry became a defining element of New York's jazz scene, setting a standard for performance excellence by which the City's musical talent would always be known. Upon hearing an advance copy of the Gershwin songbook, Ira Gershwin remarked, "I never knew how good our songs were until I heard Ella Fitzgerald sing them."

In 1959, while Fitzgerald was recording with Verve and taking top honors at the first-ever Grammy awards, a singer named Guadalupe Victoria Yoli Raymond was stunning audiences at La Red nightclub in Havana, Cuba, by uttering profanities, hitting herself, and ripping at her hair and clothing while performing. Whether she was channeling the country's political turmoil (the revolution took place that year) or some interior turbulence was unclear: **LA LUPE** (1939–1992), as she was known, lived a life of never-ending melodrama, having been left by her husband after he had an affair with the third member of their musical trio. Whatever the source, she mesmerized audiences with her Santeria-born wild cries, orgasmic shrilling, and self-flagellation (even her husband described one of her performances as resembling "an epileptic fit").

In 1962 La Lupe, by then divorced, joined many other Cuban artists in leaving the country, and she brought her dramatic performance style to New York—where male musicians from all over Latin America had already begun making a vibrant Latin music scene. Although her flamboyant, blatantly sexual performance style shocked some musicians, many of whom were classically trained and considered her behavior déclassé, her soulful singing was popular, leading to several successful records. She also collaborated with Latin jazz and mambo king Tito Puente, after which a string of hits sent her to the top of the Latin charts. Within a short time her powerful voice, uninhibited physicality, and *yiyiyi* screams earned her the title in the Latin press of "Queen of Latin Soul."

New York's Puerto Ricans, meanwhile, eagerly embraced Cuban beats. With producers eager to popularize Latin music among mainstream audiences, the name "salsa" emerged—even though purists objected to lumping together the Cuban Son, Puerto Rican bomba, and Dominican merengue. (In particular, Puente, a jazz composer and band leader who'd trained at Juilliard, repeatedly told reporters, "I am not a cook, I am a musician!") In time, however, the label stuck, and the City's Nuyoricans developed an entire salsa scene.

Unfortunately, La Lupe's wild theatrics—derided by some as camp, embraced by others as emotionally authentic—mirrored an unstable personal life that included drug addiction, a mentally ill second husband, and an inability to manage finances. When her behavior became even more erratic, Puente fired her, replacing her with Celia Cruz, who was less fiery but more reliable. As salsa developed an ever-wider following, it was Cruz—and not Lupe—who would ride the wave of the genre's popularity, eventually being crowned the "Queen of Salsa."

Meanwhile, Lupe descended into addiction and poverty, eventually suffering a back injury and a house fire before joining a Pentecostal church.

Regardless, it was La Lupe's emotional performance style and powerful, sensual, soul-infused renditions of pop classics that had paved the way for the commercial success of New York's Latin music. Many of her fans, including the filmmaker Ela Troyano, regret that La Lupe didn't receive more recognition during her lifetime. "La Lupe was an amazing artist who has never been given her due: because she was black and because her lyrics and her stance were very working class," she told me. In 2008 Troyano released a documentary aimed at restoring La Lupe's rightful place as an artist as visionary and self-empowered as Frida Kahlo. And in 2002, a stretch of East 140th Street in the Bronx was renamed "La Lupe Way."

LA LUPE

In the early 1970s, several downtown musicians began experimenting with a form of music that, instead of offering melodic emotional reassurances, aimed to fully express the angst and alienation endemic to struggling-to-survive-in-the-City. One of them, **DEBBIE HARRY** (b. 1945), who had worked as a hostess at the Playboy Club and as a waitress at Max's Kansas City, joined with her boyfriend Chris Stein and formed a band, Angel and the Snake. When they took the stage with their offbeat, unpolished songs at CBGB's, a grungy club on the Bowery that allowed new bands to incubate, they inadvertently helped kick off both the City's first real rock scene and the invention of punk.

After just a few performances, Angel and the Snake disbanded, but Harry and Stein quickly formed Blondie, named for the dismissive sobriquet strangers on the street would use to refer to Harry (and not Harry's real name, as many fans incorrectly assumed). Cowriting songs about lost love, falling apart, and wanting to die, Harry and Stein rejected the bland, everything-is-going-to-be-okay approach of mainstream songwriters; instead they penned lyrics about living in a city teetering on the edge of bankruptcy and rife with crime, poverty, and dilapidation.

Other downtown bands like Television and the Ramones similarly pushed the boundaries past anything American musicians had done before (following on the heels of nihilist 1960s group The Velvet Underground and the garish, gender-bending New York Dolls, whose burlesque tactics forged what became known as glam rock). Together, these misfits brought about an era of screaming electric guitars and raw, unvarnished lyrics that soon influenced another emerging punk scene across the pond.

Most of Blondie's songs were more traditionally composed than those of the era's other groups; this led to a record deal and play on the airwaves, part of what MTV, founded in 1981 in the City, championed as rock's New Wave. While London's Sex Pistols ultimately surpassed all the New York bands in their performed nihilism, Harry's willingness to step out of what, until then, had been a folk-driven rock paradigm was instrumental in establishing downtown's first rock scene, a morass of fractured lyrics and loud combustible sounds for which CBGB's will always be remembered.

When in 1980 Harry namechecked hip-hop pioneers Fab Five Freddy and Grandmaster Flash in Blondie's song "Rapture," it became the very first single with rap—the just-burgeoning on the streets New York art form—to top American pop charts.

Although the seeds of rap were growing in the seventies, it wasn't until the music industry figure **SYLVIA ROBINSON** (1936–2011) committed it to vinyl in 1979 that the genre of rap began its meteoric climb to mainstream consciousness.

Robinson was a successful rhythm-and-blues recording artist who briefly owned a publishing company and record label before opening a sound studio in New Jersey. One night at the Harlem World Club disco she observed the reaction on the dance floor when the deejay inventively mixed together different recorded albums, improvising rhyme overtop. The "kids were going crazy," she told an interviewer. "He would say something like, 'Throw your hands up in the air,' and they'd do it."

Wanting to push the sound out into the market, she quickly assembled a rap group; with $750, she put out the first rap single, "Rapper's Delight," the opening lines of which gave the new movement a name ("I say a hip hop, hibbit to the hibbit to the hip-hip-hop and you don't stop"). Within weeks "Rapper's Delight" had sold two million copies and created a commercial model for what had previously only existed as an unfocused—and therefore difficult to package and sell—form of street art.

She named her rap group the Sugarhill Gang, after the affluent Sugar Hill district in Harlem. Soon, as Sugar Hill Records, she and her husband, Joe, were recording other rappers, including Grandmaster Flash and the Furious Five. Despite the intensely local nature of the music—many of the songs channeled African Americans' frustration about the violence and discrimination they experienced in New York's roughest neighborhoods—the music resonated across the country.

By the mid-eighties, larger companies had big-footed Sugar Hill Records out of business. But among the rap cognoscenti, Robinson was, and will always be, the mother of hip-hop.

New York City in the eighties found Madonna honing her act at The Roxy and Danceteria, Cyndi Lauper's New Wave pop and rock on the airwaves, and the beginning of the alternative scene—this in addition to a continuation of the seventies' downtown punk scene.

These sounds, along with hip-hop, carried on through the nineties, when electronica birthed the music genres known as club and house. These styles were thriving when Rekha Malhotra, a.k.a. **DJ REKHA** (b. 1971), began infusing electronic tunes with bhangra—centuries-old celebration music from the Punjab with an impossible-to-ignore rhythmic character.

In 1997, she introduced a monthly Basement Bhangra party at SOB's nightclub on Varick Street. (Bhangra was created to celebrate the spring harvest of bhang, or hemp, and is grounded in the forceful beats of a double-headed drum.) These nights didn't just resonate with young South-Asian Americans whose parents remade the complexion of the City after passage of the Immigration and Nationality Act of 1965; they also appealed to a wide range of music- and dance-loving club-goers, with bhangra eventually wending its way into hip-hop hits by Jay Z and Missy Elliott.

Rekha's ear for house music, along with bhangra's authentic roots in Punjabi culture, both expanded the musical consciousness of New Yorkers and helped elevate New York's South Asian community into the City's pop culture scene.

THE MYTHMAKERS

Affluence and its attendant amenities and privileges have always fascinated. So it created quite a stir when in 1889 the daughter of an established New York family, whose lineage stretched back to the earliest Dutch and English settlers, began revealing the goings-on of New York's high society.

Eleven years after making her formal society debut on Fifth Avenue in 1879, **EDITH WHARTON** (1862–1937) was published by *Scribner's Magazine*; numerous short stories, essays, and book-length works of fiction followed, including *The House of Mirth* and *Ethan Frome*.

Her masterworks—like *The Age of Innocence*, which won the Pulitzer Prize—didn't just elevate the overall quality of American literature produced in this era; by chronicling the repression and hypocrisy of the affluent, as well as showing how they were affected by the forces of change in the age of mechanization, she revealed how New York's aristocrats are, in truth, just as lost and confused as everyone else.

Decades after Wharton's death in 1937, the fables she created about the beautiful, but tortured, lives of New York's gilded set have continued to endure—and are periodically reaffirmed on the stage and by Hollywood.

When **JOAN DIDION** (b. 1934), a native Californian, wrote in 1967 about the end of her love affair with New York, she too created a lasting parable, but one of a different sort.

In "Goodbye to All That," Didion took the longstanding idea of New York as the ultimate testing ground and enshrined it as "the mysterious nexus of all love and money and power, the shining and perishable dream itself." Other writers have described that battle for centuries, but Didion went further, methodically ripping off the veil of external struggle and revealing, in clear, piercing prose, the real adversary city-dwellers seek to confront and conquer: the beast within. She wrote, "[S]ome weeks I had to charge food at Bloomingdale's gourmet shop in order to eat, a fact which went unmentioned in the letters I wrote to California." And later: "I no longer had any interest in hearing about the advances other people had received from their publishers, about plays which were having second-act trouble in Philadelphia, or about people I would like very much if only I would come out and meet them. I had already met them, always."

So powerfully did her writing capture both the mesmerizing allure Manhattan has for wandering spirits and the existential despair of trying to survive in a floor-through apartment on East 75th Street that, for the next half century, saying "goodbye to all that" would become nothing less than a literary cliché.

NEW YORK WAS NO MERE
CITY. IT WAS INSTEAD AN
INFINITELY ROMANTIC
NOTION, THE MYSTERIOUS
NEXUS OF ALL LOVE AND
MONEY AND POWER, THE
SHINING AND PERISHABLE
DREAM ITSELF.

—JOAN DIDION, 1967

For more than two decades Didion and her husband, the writer John Gregory Dunne, enjoyed successful, authorly careers in Los Angeles, where they also raised a daughter, Quintana Roo.

But the final chapter of her life has provided an ironic coda to her essay: in 1988, she returned to New York, moving back to the same Upper East Side neighborhood she'd previously fled. Then, in 2003 and 2005, Didion suffered the grievous twin losses of her husband and daughter. In between, she wrote *The Year of Magical Thinking*, an astonishing National Book Award–winning memoir about her husband's death, which producer Scott Rudin asked her to adapt for the stage; in 2007, she watched Vanessa Redgrave perform her script on Broadway. Where else but in the center of power and magic could a tragedy become a book and a book become a Broadway play? Long after her parting shot, Didion proved New York remains a mysterious, powerful nexus.

THE BARBIZON HOTEL

THE ICONS

From the moment she took top prize at a singing contest at a bar in Greenwich Village in 1960, **BARBRA STREISAND** (b. 1942), a Jewish girl from Brooklyn, developed a loyal following among various groups of New Yorkers. At nightclubs, gay men adored her torch songs and impromptu one-liners; her show-stopping performance as Miss Marmelstein in *I Can Get It for You Wholesale*—when she was only nineteen—beguiled Broadway audiences; and so extraordinary was her turn in *Funny Girl* in 1964 that one drama critic declared: "If New York were Paris," Broadway could temporarily rename itself the "Rue Streisand."

Even if Hollywood and record companies took ever-so-slightly longer to warm up to what Letty Cottin Pogrebin described as Streisand's most famous character type, "the Jewish Big Mouth," ultimately it was exactly her unabashed ethnicity, her Jewish looks, her outspokenness, and her lush multiplatinum, Grammy-Emmy-Tony-Oscar-winning voice that catapulted her to iconic status. Babs's personification of a Brooklyn-bred "New Yawka" came to represent how people worldwide think of New Yorkers in general. Or, as a writer in a Jewish feminist periodical once said, "By shoving a Jewish girl's face in front of the cameras, she was announcing, beneath all the self-deprecation, *I'm here, I'm a bagel, and you're gonna learn to love me*."

Some artists express themselves in music; others in clay or paint. But few are more gifted at assembling an outfit than **IRIS APFEL** (b. 1921), an interior designer who, at the age of eighty-five, became what she refers to as "a geriatric starlet." Apfel was raised in Astoria, Queens; in her younger years, she helped run a textile company with her husband, Carl. All the while, she amassed a world-class collection of all manner of jewelry and tchotchkes. For more than six decades—seriously, *sixty years*—she was well-known among the City's design cognoscenti for using her innate style to create magnificent ensembles that blend multicultural elements into a cohesive whole. But it wasn't until the Metropolitan Museum of Art's Costume Institute featured an exhibit of her outfits in 2005 that Coach, Kate Spade, Finlandia Vodka, and MAC Cosmetics asked her to star in ad campaigns— publicity that soon generated a book and an Albert Maysles documentary.

Still going strong in her mid-nineties, and still wearing her signature saucer-sized glasses, Iris—among the chosen few with single-name status— continues to prove why charm and wit remain the most attractive of all accessories. Responding to a question from the writer Taffy Brodesser-Akner, Iris replied, "No matter how marvelous" an outfit is, "if you're not comfortable with it . . . you're gonna look like a jerk." Given a choice, "it's better to be unstylish but happy."

Wit is, perhaps, the most prized of all traits among sophisticates. Rarely has it existed in greater abundance than among the Algonquin Round Table, the name for a group of writers, editors, actors, and publicists who famously convened at the "Gonk" hotel during the Prohibition era to swap stories, make merry, and collaborate on creative projects.

But even among New York's creative elites, the writer, poet, and mistress of bon mots **DOROTHY PARKER** (1893–1967) stood out for her rapier dialogue and machine-gunned one-liners. Parker joined *The New Yorker* at its inception in 1925, ultimately contributing more than one hundred book reviews, profiles, poems, and short stories to the magazine. She was known as much for her searing takedowns of those in power as for her darkly comical views. Both qualities were present in much of her writing, especially in her unforgettable wisecracks, like "Brevity is the soul of lingerie" or "Beauty is only skin deep, but ugly goes clean to the bone." But she also wrote about deeper concerns, like in "Arrangement in Black and White," a short story from 1927 that mocked the hypocrisy of prejudiced whites.

Though Parker was often successful at wringing humor from pain—as in, "I'd rather have a bottle in front of me than a frontal lobotomy"—she waged a ferocious battle with depression, which in its reign included alcoholism and

DOROTHY PARKER

several suicide attempts. Social inequality and prejudice were major sources of the pain she felt; she once told an interviewer that what disturbed her most about America was injustice, intolerance, stupidity, and segregation.

She worked to mitigate that pain by promoting social justice. In the 1930s she raised money in support of the Scottsboro Boys (black Alabama teenagers wrongly convicted and sentenced to death for allegedly raping two white women); in 1950 she defended Paul Robeson when he was banned from television; and, upon her death at age seventy-three, she left her entire estate to Dr. Martin Luther King Jr.

Still, it was her bon mots that personified New York wit and continue to delight. These include numerous phrases now in common usage (such as "what the hell") and ditties like this timeless tribute to human suffering, titled "Resumé":

RAZORS PAIN YOU,

RIVERS ARE DAMP,

ACIDS STAIN YOU,

AND DRUGS CAUSE CRAMP.

GUNS AREN'T LAWFUL,

NOOSES GIVE,

GAS SMELLS AWFUL.

YOU MIGHT AS WELL LIVE.

Several years after Parker died in her Upper East Side hotel suite, another witty, cynical character sought refuge in the City from the torment of suburban life in Morristown, New Jersey. To survive on her own after arriving as a teenager, **FRAN LEBOWITZ** (b. 1950) started out driving a taxi and writing pornography, but she ultimately couldn't help but follow her natural-born profession as a writer and social critic—even if she would become more well-known for all the writing she avoided than what she produced. "I write so slowly," she once said, "that I could write in my own blood without hurting myself."

The first editor to hire Lebowitz was pop art and nightlife impresario Andy Warhol, who gave her a gig as a columnist for *Interview* magazine. Soon after, she published two essay collections: *Metropolitan Life* (1978) and *Social Studies* (1981), both steeped in her cosmopolitan, New York viewpoint. But it was her outspoken judgmentalism, endless supply of sardonic wit, and unabashed butch lesbian appearance that rendered her the embodiment of 1970s cool—a personification that lasted into, and was still being exalted in, the twenty-first century.

Thirty years, a title on *Vanity Fair*'s masthead, and scores of public appearances later, Lebowitz's publisher is still waiting for her third book. (In the meantime, Vintage Books compiled her previous two volumes into *The Fran Lebowitz Reader* in 1994.) Despite the dearth of printed output, Lebowitz—who describes herself as "the outstanding waster of time of my generation"—occupies such a unique, only-in-New-York role that Martin Scorsese created the 2010 documentary *Public Speaking* to showcase her talents as a conversationalist.

"You start with a topic, and then she would riff, like a jazz performer," Mr. Scorsese said. "It's in the timing, the telling of the story, the punchlines, the pauses, that's the music, see. That's the writing."

It's for her conversational virtuosity that her friend Graydon Carter, longtime editor of *Vanity Fair*, has remained her steadfast patron. Through her talks, which she delivers nationwide, she continues to serve as New York's erstwhile counterculture ambassador.

"Everyone says New York has changed tremendously but unfortunately I have not," Lebowitz gushed forth to me in March 2016. "It's not the New York I came to." Asked whether she had ever considered leaving, she had a quick reply: "Where else would you live? Every place else is Atlanta."

WHEN YOU LEAVE
NEW YORK, YOU
ARE ASTONISHED
AT HOW CLEAN
THE REST OF THE
WORLD IS. CLEAN
IS NOT ENOUGH.

—FRAN LEBOWITZ, 1978

THE EDUCATORS

In the early days of the republic, when it came to education, privileged white men concerned themselves with sending their sons to Kings College (now Columbia University, founded in 1754 by royal charter of King George II of England). Fortunately for the remaining youngsters, there were some women who recognized the importance of giving *all* children the tools necessary to grow into thriving adults.

An example: **CATHERINE "KATY" FERGUSON** (1774–1854) was a cake baker who took notice of the orphaned white and black children roaming the streets near her residence in lower Manhattan. When she was about nineteen she began inviting them into her home every Sunday for rudimentary lessons—and one need look no further than her own background to understand her impulse in doing so. According to Lewis Tappan, a prominent merchant and founder of the American Anti-Slavery Society who interviewed Ferguson in 1850, she was born to a Virginia woman held in the bonds of slavery; when she was just eight years old, her mother was sold off by her master, and lost to Katy forever.

Although Ferguson, still a teenager herself, had never learned to read or write, she taught the children the life skills and scripture her mother had taught to her in her youngest years. Then, when a minister at a nearby church learned of her efforts, he invited her to move the meetings into the church basement. In Tappan's view, Ferguson deserved to be credited with establishing the first Sunday School in the City.

In 1801, a group of female Quakers—the name for members of the Christian denomination known as the Religious Society of Friends—likewise took notice of the youngsters of all backgrounds who weren't being helped by existing charities. Earlier, **CATHARINE BOWNE MURRAY** (1758–1819), who married into the clan of Murrays of Murray Hill fame, had invited the others to gather at her home, where they formed the the Association of Women Friends for the Relief of the Poor (commonly referred to as the "Female Association"). Their focus was on providing education to any boy or girl "whose parents belong to no religious society, and who, from some cause or other, cannot be admitted into any of the charity schools of this city."

This notion—that *all* children of the City deserved education regardless of sex, race, creed, or their parents' finances or religious observance—was incalculably significant. Until then, most adults had only seen fit to teach youngsters who were members of their own ethnic or religious groups.

By working with the concept that education could exist independent of religious groups or racial identity, these women laid the foundation for a uniform system of education that, in theory, offered *every* individual opportunity for advancement—which is the very heart of the American dream. It also established the concept of NYC as melting pot: No matter what a person looked like, or from where one came, or from whose womb one emerged, in the eyes of these women, every child was potential-in-waiting. This conception of education established the principle on which the largest public school system in the nation would eventually be built.

Prior to the formation of the Female Association, education in the City consisted of an array of individual efforts. Affluent families hired tutors to instruct their children at home. Churches established charity schools for poor members of the faith. And, in 1794, a group of well-to-do white men who advocated for the full abolition of slavery—including John Jay and Alexander Hamilton—established the African Free School, a one-room schoolhouse on Cliff Street that used donations to provide schooling for about forty Black students.

When in June 1801, the Female Association opened its first co-ed public school, it combined elements of those different efforts into one approach. Pooling their resources, the women rented a room for the school and, according to a Friends history given by William H.S. Wood in 1902, hired "a widow woman of good education and morals as instructor."

Four years later, in 1805, Mayor DeWitt Clinton convened the New York Free School Society, a group aimed at providing a free education to the City's children—by which the participants actually meant NYC's Caucasian boys. For many years, the group looked to the Female Association for assistance establishing and running schools for boys—and began providing them with public funds to keep teaching the girls. (When the Female Association opened its second school soon after, it was exclusively for girls.)

In 1825, all of the groups were folded together under the name the Public School Society; this would later be reorganized in 1842 under the Board of Education. By 1871, the NYC Board of Education served more than 35,000 children at eighty-nine grammar schools, where the vast majority of teachers were female—an arrangement that persists today. Of the City's approximately 76,000 teachers in 2016, more than 75 percent are women.

"The whole public school system rests on the work of women," the eminent historian of education Diane Ravitch told me. Although in the early years the names on all the records were men, she added, "the whole schooling of public schoolchildren—millions of children—always rested on the backs of women."

⋀ ⋁

Even after nineteenth-century New York had, at least on paper, embraced the idea of educating all children, there proved another significant obstacle to educating even the Caucasian kids who made up the bulk of the City's poor youth: their parents.

Most poor immigrants, and especially those who came to New York from rural peasant communities in Europe, relied on their children to work to bring in money for the family. Unsure of how they'd get their next meal, many parents had a hard time fathoming how giving up potential wages could ultimately benefit the

IT SEEMED TO ME THAT
IF WE COULD KEEP [THE
DESIRE TO LEARN] ALIVE
THROUGH CHILDHOOD
AND INTO ADULT LIFE, WE
WOULD RELEASE A FORCE
MORE PRECIOUS AND
POWERFUL FOR GOOD
THAN ANY PHYSICAL
FORCE THE SCIENTISTS
EVER DISCOVERED.

—CAROLINE PRATT, 1948

and forests she enjoyed as a child, Pratt began looking for alternative ways of teaching that would similarly give students opportunities to learn from real experiences. She believed in offering children opportunities to encounter frustrations and setbacks, which, when overcome, provided both valuable lessons and a sense of self-empowerment.

By 1913, Pratt, who lived and socialized among other progressive thinkers in the Village, was convinced that learning occurred best through creative play with open-ended materials. She envisioned a classroom that allowed for children's self-directed planning and problem solving, augmented by field trips and activities that permitted children to participate in authentic social interactions with other members of their community.

The benefits of learning from one's own doing had been reinforced for her during a trip to Sweden, where Pratt observed "Educational sloyd," a learning practice of utilizing woodworking and other handicrafts to foster critical-thinking skills in children. She spent many hours observing children happily immersed in creative play, in which they were naturally driven to think carefully before acting, and thereby would develop a strong interior sense of responsibility and judgment.

Devising a new approach to what "school" could mean, Pratt founded the Play School in 1914 in a three-room apartment in Greenwich Village; soon after it was renamed the City and Country School and was moved to larger quarters on West 12th Street.

To facilitate the creative play she determined was so important, Pratt devised two sets of blocks that would allow children to freely construct structures and engage in dramatic play of their own design, whether indoors or out: indoor wooden unit blocks of corresponding measurement that led children to intuit math relationships and provided the foundation for lessons in collaborative problem-solving, and large outdoor blocks that required lifting, carrying, pushing, and pulling, sometimes by more than one student, to strengthen gross motor skills and foster a need for social interaction.

In time, Pratt's blocks would become a staple of classrooms all over the City, and the breadth of their educational benefits would become known across America and beyond. However, it wasn't until 1947—when Pratt was eighty—that the educator known for favoring human interaction over worship of books would begin setting down her philosophy in writing. The name of her volume, published in 1948 when she was eighty-one: "*I Learn From Children: An Adventure in Progressive Education.*"

⁂

In 1916, teacher **LUCY SPRAGUE MITCHELL** (1878–1967) cofounded the Bureau of Educational Experiments. There she and a staff of teachers and researchers carefully observed how preschool-aged children interacted with their teachers and classroom materials in order to "find out what kind of environment is best suited to [children's] learning and growth, to create that environment, and to train adults to maintain it." Through these observations Mitchell developed a strong belief in experiential rather than passive learning. From there she opened a nursery school with an affiliated training center for teachers. In 1950, this center was renamed Bank Street College of Education, which still trains teachers to be sensitive to the delicate interplay between the emotional, intellectual, and psychological aspects of children's development.

After several years teaching in public school, **ELISABETH IRWIN** (1880–1942), a psychologist and social worker, became outraged by the widespread practice of what was then called "retardation": the holding back of students who failed to perform as well as their peers.

With as much as 30 or 40 percent of students in a single classroom facing retention each year—according to Nicholas O'Han, an historian who works at Irwin's school—this practice had become so common that the situation had reached crisis proportions. "There they sat, thousands of students often two and three years older than their age-appropriate classmates, often off in a corner—'the old dunce-cap atrocity,'" Irwin called it.

The greatest tragedy, Irwin felt, was the deleterious effects suffered by the students, which included damage to self-esteem as well as truancy—internalizing the message that they were somehow inferior, or that there was no point in continuing, many students simply elected to drop out. So Irwin decided to find out more for herself. After administering intelligence tests to these students, often discovering in them comparable—and in some cases, "superior"—intelligence, she came to believe that, instead of imposing authoritarian demands, teachers should instead work to meet the needs of individual students.

In 1921, Irwin founded the Little Red School, an alternative public elementary school where children were offered instruction that allowed them to proceed at their own pace—without being subject to reprimand or shaming. "Threats of all kinds were taboo," Irwin once explained. "Children were treated humanely, respectfully, and firmly. Above all, they were treated not as little adults, but as children, each one a unique moral, mental, and creative agent, and each one expected to be a contributing member of the classroom community."

Seventy years after Little Red opened, the eminent scholar bell hooks, writing in *Teaching to Transgress: Education as the Practice of Freedom*, captured what is essentially the same philosophy: a classroom is a "location of possibility" where "we have the opportunity to labor for freedom, to demand of ourselves and our comrades an openness of mind and heart that allows us to face reality even as we collectively imagine ways to move beyond boundaries."

THE POLITICOS

In the 1950s, when the Democratic Party was dominated by white men, **SHIRLEY CHISHOLM** (1924–2005) decided it was time for the progressive party to do a better job of representing black New Yorkers.

Born in Bedford-Stuyvesant, Chisholm was the daughter of a factory laborer from Guyana and a domestic worker from Barbados. She first became interested in politics during college. After earning a master's degree in early childhood education from Teachers College, Columbia University, she joined a Democratic clubhouse in Brooklyn, helped to elect Brooklyn's first African American municipal court judge, and cofounded the Bedford-Stuyvesant Political League, a group aimed at bolstering political participation among African Americans.

But Chisholm didn't just talk the talk; she walked the walk. In 1964, the outspoken but always dignified Chisholm won a seat in the New York State Assembly, where she worked on issues like extending unemployment benefits to domestic workers, protecting tenure rights of teachers during pregnancy, and promoting assistance to poor students for college.

After a court-ordered redistricting finally gave Bed-Stuy its own congressional district, in 1968 Chisholm ran for Congress, campaigning with the slogan "Unbought and Unbossed." From a sound truck parked in front of housing projects, she'd announce: "Ladies and gentlemen . . . this is Fighting Shirley Chisholm."

She won, making her the first African American woman elected to the U.S. Congress. She then took her forthright style to Washington, where she backed numerous bills to help women and minorities and was a founding member of both the Black Caucus and the National Women's Political Caucus (NWPC).

In 1972, even though she knew she stood little chance of winning her party's nomination, Chisholm declared her candidacy for the presidency. Despite few funds, a short campaign, and no support from party machinery, she got on the ballot in fourteen states and received more than 150 votes at the Democratic National Convention.

"The next time a woman runs, or a black, or a Jew, or anyone from a group that the country is 'not ready' to elect to its highest office," Chisholm later wrote of her unsuccessful bid, "I believe that he or she will be taken seriously from the start. . . . I ran because someone had to do it first."

No matter what office Chisholm held, she had a singular goal: to ensure the government was accountable to all citizens, not just white ones. "There are people in our country's history who don't look left or right, they just look straight ahead," said President Barack Obama upon posthumously awarding the Presidential Medal of Freedom to Chisholm in 2015. "Shirley Chisholm was one of those people."

SHIRLEY CHISHOLM

While Chisholm was unfailingly courteous, Bronx native **BELLA ABZUG** (1920–1998), a lifelong lefty with a loud, gravelly voice and a penchant for wide-brimmed hats, was so brash she earned the nickname "Battling Bella."

"If you combined Churchill, Oprah, Dr. Ruth, and Emma Goldman, you'd get a picture of Bella," Gloria Steinem once said about her friend.

As a preteen, Abzug, the academically gifted second daughter of Russian Jewish émigrés, stood on the street soliciting donations for a Labor Zionist youth group. In her adult years, she spent a quarter century as a political activist and labor lawyer until, at the age of fifty, she decided she wanted to represent the City in Washington. And so, in 1970, she ran for Congress.

Having cofounded and run both Women Strike for Peace and the Coalition for a Democratic Alternative, she channeled antiwar sentiment into an upset victory over the Democratic incumbent in the 1970 primary, becoming both the first Jewish woman ever elected to Congress and the first person ever elected on a women's rights/peace platform.

In Washington, Abzug spearheaded many of the policies that future generations of women would take for granted, like the Equal Credit Opportunity Act (ECOA), which gives women fair access to consumer credit, and Title IX regulations, which prohibit educational institutions receiving federal money from discriminating on the basis of gender. She also introduced an amendment to expand the 1964 Civil Rights Act to include protection for gays and lesbians;

IF THEY DON'T GIVE YOU A SEAT AT THE TABLE, BRING IN A FOLDING CHAIR.

—SHIRLEY CHISHOLM, 1984

coauthored the Freedom of Information Act, which provides the public access to government records; and wrote what came to be known as the Clean Water Act, one of the nation's first and most influential environmental laws.

Abzug's career as an elected official ended in 1976 when she left the House to run for the Senate and lost by a fraction of a percentage point. But she continued to campaign, first for mayor of New York City (traversing the boroughs in a yellow Chevrolet Impala convertible), and, later, in two more failed congressional bids.

By stepping up to the microphone and demanding that Washington address women's needs, Abzug made it acceptable for other second-wave feminists in New York (and beyond) to assert, rather than request, their legal entitlements. And by frequently—and unapologetically—deploying blunt and colorful language, she fueled the stereotype of New Yorkers as being brash and aggressive.

While Abzug's shrewd political maneuverings produced many tangible improvements for the City (including significant funds to maintain the subways), her legacy is perhaps best summed up by comments she made to *The New York Times* during her very first race: "[W]e've got to get out there and raise holy hell."

Holy hell might be an appropriate description of the public drubbing that **GERALDINE A. FERRARO** (1935–2011), a former congresswoman from Queens, received in 1984 when she became the first woman in U.S. history nominated for national office by a major political party.

An Italian American who was encouraged to join politics by longtime New York governor Mario Cuomo, Ferraro's down-to-earth personality and image as a devoted mother from a blue-collar family led Democrats to believe she could help Walter F. Mondale win votes. And, indeed, her spirited personality, confidence in standing up to frequently condescending male opponents, and pragmatic approach to abortion (she consistently supported women's right to choose while acknowledging that she opposed the procedure personally) propelled her to national prominence.

But with the enormous popularity of the incumbent Reagan-Bush ticket, and given the cloud of questions that arose after her husband initially refused to release his tax returns—and how their accumulated wealth, once revealed, undermined her working-class image—their campaign to enter the White House fizzled.

For New Yorkers, however, Ferraro's political career was a resounding success. Having lost her father when she was eight, she had grown up the product of a single mother who earned a living working as a seamstress. She later attended law school at night while working as a public school teacher; once her children were in school, she became a Queens assistant district attorney. For five years she investigated rape, domestic violence, and crimes against the elderly, growing ever more frustrated by the challenges working people face.

In 1978, she won a seat in Congress, then utilized an assignment to the Public Works and Transportation Committee to win support for improving mass transit near LaGuardia Airport. Although the bulk of her constituents came from Archie Bunker territory—in deference to those constituents, she sometimes supported conservative legislation—she frequently pushed back against Reagan administration policies that she viewed as harmful to those in her district. In particular she fought to minimize budget cuts that devastated public schools, libraries, and hospitals and sponsored legislation reforms that would be more economically supportive of women. This included, most notably, an act that ultimately resulted in the historic health insurance continuation program now known as COBRA.

While Ferraro's nomination didn't get her all the way to the Oval Office, it did bring women a few steps closer; it took another twenty-four years before a woman would again run on a major party's national ticket—Sarah Palin as running mate for John McCain—and another eight years for a woman to finally win enough major party delegates to be nominated for president: Hillary Rodham Clinton in 2016. And it confirmed the role of New York in providing political leadership for the national stage, something that began with the country's founding in the eighteenth century and continues today.

THE

PRESERVATIONISTS

As a reporter for an architecture magazine in the 1950s, **JANE JACOBS** (1916–2006) found herself regularly confounded by the City's efforts at "urban renewal," which consisted of bulldozing so-called slums and replacing them with large, sterile new building complexes that felt unwelcoming and usually failed to attract either people or commerce. She began talking to residents of East Harlem about the specifics of what was and was not needed to improve their lives; from their conversations she realized that most planners, while steeped in academic theory, had not invested any time in understanding the nitty-gritty details of neighborhood functioning.

The result was her 1961 masterwork, *The Death and Life of Great American Cities*. Her book didn't just shake the foundations of urban planning and provide a new blueprint for rebuilding cities; it also touched off an eventual backlash against Robert Moses, the planning czar who had for decades led massive construction projects throughout the City—causing a significant amount of neighborhood demolition.

Those in power at the time typically believed that cities benefitted from more open space, lower population density, and the construction of large buildings— which was essentially polite speak for the view that congested, working-class neighborhoods were nothing more than visual eyesores and breeding grounds for trouble. Jacobs, however, cogently argued that population density and diverse, mixed-use buildings were essential for the organic intermingling of residents that gives rise to vibrant, vital neighborhoods. She wrote that urban neighborhoods, like complex ecosystems, are a series of ever-changing, untidy interactions between people and space, interactions that provide "eyes on the street"—people of all ages and classes coming and going at different times of day and night. This density of observers, she concluded, provides not only safety but a shared sense of responsibility for community well-being—an idea that would later come to be known as "social capital" and considered of paramount importance to economists and political scientists.

When Moses's plans for the Lower Manhattan Expressway threatened to cut through Washington Square Park and her own beloved Greenwich Village neighborhood, Jacobs spearheaded a committee to stop it. She arranged and participated in multiple protests, for which she was arrested at least twice.

Despite how planners and the architectural academe excoriated her treatise— and her—when *The Death and Life of Great American Cities* came out, the book became required reading in universities worldwide. And despite Moses's seemingly unstoppable power—known as the "master builder," he was ultimately responsible for billions of dollars of bridges and towers and arenas and highways, including the Cross Bronx Expressway, which displaced millions of city-dwellers—Jacobs's people-power won out, and the City's congested, beloved Greenwich Village and Washington Square Park remain a central part of downtown life today.

In 1963, an editor for *The New York Times* created a post specifically for another talented writer, ADA LOUISE HUXTABLE (1921–2013). As the *Times's* first architecture critic, Huxtable wrote fierce, passionate critiques of various projects throughout the City, championing the importance of historic buildings that played an ongoing role in modern life.

So powerful were her critiques that an approval or rejection from Huxtable could determine a project's fate. And her ability to astutely distill the nuances of the built environment in the context of city life put a concern for architecture and city planning into popular consciousness in a way it had never been before—and may never be again. Her persuasive writing was a driving force in the 1965 establishment of the New York City Landmarks Preservation Commission, which empowered the City to prevent destruction or deformation of significant properties and neighborhoods, even when privately owned.

As Huxtable loved to be dazzled by architecture, she was a champion of architects willing to take risks and make bold statements—and yet, at the same time she shared a Jacobsian concern for city-dwellers. She celebrated projects that promoted the "urban greatness" of the City, like the installation of a steel sculpture by Isamu Noguchi in Lower Manhattan, and condemned those she felt were "too facile and empty to be called architecture at all."

Without fail, Huxtable championed the City above politics, developers, and investors. Her devotion to NYC was such that she "took architectural insults to her

THERE IS NO LOGIC THAT
CAN BE SUPERIMPOSED
ON THE CITY; PEOPLE
MAKE IT, AND IT IS TO
THEM, NOT BUILDINGS,
THAT WE MUST FIT
OUR PLANS.

—JANE JACOBS, 1961

city personally," noted the architecture critic Alexandra Lange. And she captured the majesty and magic of the built city in a way that forced developers to consider the philosophical—and not just financial—implications of their work.

"When it is good, New York is very, very good," she wrote in 1968. "Which is why New Yorkers put up with so much that is bad. When it is good, this is a city of fantastic strength, sophistication, and beauty. It is like no other city in time or place. [It fills us with] awe in the presence of massed, concentrated steel, stone, power, and life."

Following the 1963 assassination of her husband, President John F. Kennedy, **JACQUELINE KENNEDY ONASSIS** (1929–1994), who had a long-standing interest in arts and preservation, moved to Fifth Avenue with her two children, where she would live for years to come. (In 1968 she married Greek shipping tycoon Aristotle Onassis, who died in 1975.)

In New York, she resumed her writing career as a book editor (begun before her first marriage), raised her kids, and continued to inspire devotion as a fashion icon. Then, when Grand Central Terminal was threatened with demolition, the former First Lady entered the arena of activism: under the auspices of the Municipal Art Society, in 1975 she headed the Committee to Save Grand Central Station and fought against Penn Central Transportation Company's proposal to replace it with a tower, becoming the public face of a campaign that ultimately wound up before the Supreme Court. Onassis's side prevailed, and the majestic, iconic terminal survived. Then, an extensive cleaning and restoration by hand in 1996 returned the painted celestial ceiling to its magnificent original splendor.

In 1982, when Lever House—an early glass skyscraper designed by Skidmore, Owings & Merrill on Park Avenue at 51st Street—was threatened, she stepped in as well, orchestrating a meeting at City Hall with Comptroller Jay Goldin, who held the deciding vote on the building's landmark status, and who she'd heard wanted a photo op. At the conclusion of the meeting she walked him out to the City Hall steps where paparazzi awaited and gave him a peck on the cheek; the next day all the tabloids ran the photo, one with the headline "The Kiss That Saved Lever House."

Again and again, Onassis stepped in to support the preservation and restoration of old buildings. Since her death in 1994, the Municipal Art Society has bestowed an annual medal in her name to individuals who make "an extraordinary impact on the quality of New York's built environment," those who are devoted to the same principle that drove Onassis: "a more glorious New York City."

In the mid-seventies, when the City was on the verge of bankruptcy, Central Park was a scary place: most surfaces were marred by graffiti, vandalism had closed the

Belvedere Castle, benches and lights were broken, the lake littered with beer cans, its lawns turned to dust. That's when **ELIZABETH BARLOW ROGERS** (b. 1936) stepped in. An expert on the City's parks and wetlands, and author of a book about Frederick Law Olmsted (Central Park's codesigner, with Calvert Vaux), she began organizing volunteer clean-up groups and raising private funds to pay for repairs.

In 1979, Mayor Ed Koch appointed her as administrator to the park; when she succeeded the following year in cofounding the Central Park Conservancy, a private organization, she became its leader. As such, 1980 was the first time since the park's founding that a single individual was responsible for all its management and maintenance. She told me, "People always say 'I don't know how I could live in New York without the park,' and I totally agree."

Rogers's first major act was to oversee an exhaustive, three-year study of all aspects of the park, from soil conditions to traffic patterns; next, she produced a comprehensive master plan for a "systematic and coherent renovation over a fifteen-year period." In addition to the nuts and bolts of the project, she argued that landscape design "is as much a part of our heritage as painting and sculpture" is, and that the park "should be treated like any other cultural institution, like any museum, botanical garden, zoological society."

Her vision was so practical and persuasive, it captured the necessary financial support to make most of it a reality; by the end of the 1980s, Central Park had become a place for locals and visitors to stretch out on Sheep Meadow and dine at the boathouse—while also serving as a backdrop for films about urban elegance and romance (instead of mugging jokes). It is true that naysayers decry the decision to allow private-interest control over public spaces—an issue that continues to affect municipalities the world over; today the CPC provides 75 percent of the park's annual $65 million operating budget. But no one disputes that Rogers's vision, organizational skills, and fund-raising abilities allowed the park to remain the City's crowning jewel into another century. Today, after taking a walk through the park every morning, she runs the nonprofit Foundation for Landscape Studies, an organization devoted to fostering what she describes as "an active understanding of the importance of place in human life."

THE

COUNTERCULTURISTS

Maybe it was her physician father's interest in the bodily expression of human behavior and feeling. Maybe it was the collision of ballet and folk dances from around the world she learned at Denishawn, the dance company in Los Angeles she attended in her early twenties. Or maybe the seeds of experimentation existed in her DNA. Whatever the source, after **MARTHA GRAHAM** (1894–1991) made her debut in New York as an independent artist in 1926, the City and the dance world were forever changed.

Before that moment Graham spent several years dancing in the Greenwich Village Follies revue and earning extra money teaching classes at the Eastman School of Music in Rochester, New York. Then, wanting to experiment with using the body as a form of lyrical expression, she opened a small studio in Greenwich Village, the Martha Graham Center of Contemporary Dance, and quickly attracted other dancers.

Instead of practicing and teaching traditional folk dances or ballet, both of which followed long-established patterns of movement, Graham began developing a new language around the basic actions of the human form, focusing not on ornate details but on elemental movements, especially contraction and release. Starting with how breath is experienced during different emotions, she created a vocabulary of gestures to express a wide array of human experiences, thereby establishing the first significant alternative to the idiom of classical ballet. And as other dancers learned and embraced this form of movement—which in time formally became known as the genre of modern dance—legions of the City's dancers would follow in her footsteps.

On April 18, 1926, Graham gave her first independent concert at the Forty-Eighth Street Theatre, which she rented with borrowed money, and shocked the audience with radical movements like spiral twists, asymmetrical balances, and a wide variety of falls. These and several of her other early works, which were devoid of the elaborate sets and costumes common to most ballet and folk productions, were often found by New York critics and audiences to be stark, obscure—even ugly.

In later performances, she incorporated avant-garde music and minimalist sculpture—fruit of collaboration with the Japanese American sculptor Isamu Noguchi. As her choreography and personal practice became more sophisticated, she created social commentaries on American life, exploring political, psychological, and sexual themes.

Over sixty-six years of teaching, choreographing, and directly running her company, Graham influenced scores of City choreographers and dancers, including Twyla Tharp, Merce Cunningham, and Paul Taylor, thereby establishing NYC as the country's epicenter of modern dance. She also paved the way for what seems to be the only other invention of an entire idiom of movement—by the action choreographer Elizabeth Streb—who began work in the 1960s and continues to develop her repertoire of "extreme action" at the Streb Lab for Action Mechanics in Williamsburg, Brooklyn.

⁂

By the 1950s, New York native **DIANE ARBUS** (1923–1971) (pronounced DEE-ann ARE-bus) had become a successful fashion photography shoot stylist, working in partnership with her husband, Allan, and seeing her work printed in publications like *Vogue*. But wanting to cultivate her own photography, Arbus, who grew up in an affluent family and attended the prestigious Fieldston school, began exploring many unglamorous locales throughout the City, where she found herself fascinated by society's outcasts.

In the City's seedy motels, public parks, mental institutions, Coney Island circus tents and freak shows, even a morgue, she befriended the downtrodden and deformed—those from whom most people usually avert their eyes—and celebrated their uniqueness in carefully considered photographs. Her subjects included a smoking transvestite in curlers, a Jewish giant at home with his parents, a smiling Mexican dwarf in his hotel room, and a set of matching twins with eerily dissimilar expressions.

In 1963 and 1966 she won Guggenheim Fellowships. In 1967, her work was featured with that of two other photographers in *New Documents*, a landmark exhibition at MoMA celebrating the willingness to face and honor components of the human experience usually considered taboo.

MOST PEOPLE GO
THROUGH LIFE DREADING
THEY'LL HAVE A TRAUMATIC
EXPERIENCE. FREAKS WERE
BORN WITH THEIR TRAUMA.
THEY'VE ALREADY PASSED
THEIR TEST IN LIFE.
THEY'RE ARISTOCRATS.

—DIANE ARBUS, 1970

Beset throughout her life with the travails of mental illness, Arbus completed suicide in July 1971 at the age of forty-eight. For decades after, critics questioned whether her work constituted a form of exploitation, or if it possibly revealed something about her internal struggles with depression.

But many others, including Arbus's daughter Doon, who became the caretaker of her mother's estate, believed those critics missed her essential idea: that the images should stand on their own, therein forcing viewers to reflect on how society does or does not accept those whose physical appearance falls outside the mainstream. In doing so, the images, which became known throughout the world, also celebrate New York as a home for so many marginalized people.

The year before her death, while teaching a photography class in 1970 at the artists' residence Westbeth, located on the western reaches of Greenwich Village, Arbus explained the beauty she found in misfits. "There's a quality of legend about freaks," she told her students. "Like a person in a fairy tale who stops you and demands that you answer a riddle. Most people go through life dreading they'll have a traumatic experience. Freaks were born with their trauma. They've already passed their test in life. They're aristocrats."

In 1961, when her aspiring playwright brother needed an audience for his work, **ELLEN STEWART** (1919–2011) transformed a basement on East 9th Street into a makeshift theater and entreated passersby to come in and watch. Stewart, who had an eye for fashion and worked at Saks Fifth Avenue designing clothes, had been nicknamed "Mama" by the Eastern European seamstresses who worked for her, which led to someone suggesting the "theater"—which had a dirt floor and sat just twenty-five people—be named La MaMa.

The name stuck even after her effort grew from a single gesture of kindness into an underground club, which in time became an essential platform for emerging artists in New York's theater scene. But, soon after first opening in 1961—when Stewart's primarily white neighbors, alarmed by the number and variety of white men visiting a black woman in the basement, complained to the authorities—the City cited fire code violations and shut her down.

Instead of giving up, Stewart, an African American with a striking, deep voice and colorful personality, moved to a loft on Second Avenue. As her endeavors proceeded, she found so much satisfaction in helping new playwrights see their work come to fruition that she quit her job at Saks Fifth Avenue so she could devote herself full-time to their cause. But, lacking funds to transform spaces to meet NYC codes, City officials shut her down again—and arrested her twice.

With her indefatigable spirit, Stewart obtained nonprofit status, then grants from the Ford, Rockefeller, and Doris Duke Foundations, which in 1968 allowed the still-always-cash-strapped theater to settle into a former meatpacking plant on East Fourth Street, where Stewart could finally hang a sign and operate legally without fear of being shut down.

Stewart's intimate forum allowed an endless parade of aspiring creatives with nowhere else to turn to experiment with writing styles, performance techniques, and even the audience's relationship to the theatergoer. Perhaps just as important, Stewart routinely supported these artists (who, starting in the twenty-first century, were crudely referred to as "content providers," but whom Stewart called her "children") in various ways. She personally introduced the performances, allowed dramatists to tackle any subject they wished, and endlessly entreated audience members to donate money. She even sometimes provided them with a place to sleep (on the couch in her apartment or in the theater) or do their laundry.

The result: La MaMa became the cornerstone of what came to be called "off-off Broadway," which changed the course of American theater.

Over the years, a significant number of major players in the City's theater scene developed or debuted work at La MaMa, including Sam Shepard, Lanford Wilson, Harvey Fierstein, Tom O'Horgan (who helped create the rock musical *Hair*), and Joseph Papp, who would later found New York's Shakespeare in the Park and The Public Theater.

Among the actors to perform on La MaMa's stage in the 1960s and 1970s were Diane Lane, Robert De Niro, and Al Pacino. Stewart also provided an early home for such visionaries as Meredith Monk, the genre-bending composer, singer, choreographer, and filmmaker; Richard Foreman, founder of the Ontological-Hysteric Theater; and Blue Man Group. Over the years, Stewart expanded the breadth of La MaMa's offerings by opening her doors to foreign theater groups, thus further enlivening the entire New York cultural scene.

In 1985, Stewart received the MacArthur Foundation "Genius" award. In 1993, owing to her significance in New York theater—doubly remarkable given

the dearth of women or blacks when she started—she became the first off-off Broadway producer inducted into the Broadway Theatre Hall of Fame.

⁂

The artist, poet, and musician **PATTI SMITH** (b. 1946) had no idea what she was doing in 1967 when she dropped out of a teachers college in New Jersey and moved to New York. There, she joined forces with kindred wandering spirit (and future art photographer) Robert Mapplethorpe, after encountering him for the second time in an East Village park.

For several years she was one of any number of drifting, mesmerized, penniless dreamers feeding off the City's creative energy while trying to eke out an existence. She restocked books at the Strand and occasionally resorted to shoplifting art supplies from Jake's when she had only enough money for a grilled cheese.

But at some point she began wanting to infuse the poetry she endlessly scribbled in notebooks with, as she would later describe, the "immediacy and frontal attack of rock and roll." So when in 1971 Mapplethorpe arranged for her to give a reading at an event organized by the Poetry Project, she was spurred into action. She asked Lenny Kaye, a guitarist who worked at the Village Oldies record store (later renamed Bleecker Bob's), if he could "play a car crash with an electric guitar." He said yes.

PATTI SMITH

SOME OF
US ARE BORN
REBELLIOUS.

—PATTI SMITH, 2010

Taking the stage at St. Mark's Church-in-the-Bowery, where the crowd included Lou Reed, Andy Warhol, and Todd Rundgren, firebrand Smith delivered a performance that both crystallized the punk spirit of the era and immediately established her cred among the City's countercultural prophets.

CREEM magazine published a suite of her poems. She began writing freelance for *Rolling Stone*. She got a gig at Max's Kansas City, then formed her own band and wrote a song with Bruce Springsteen. In 1975 she played a two-month residency at CBGB's with Richard Hell's band Television and debuted her first album.

After spending most of the 1980s out of the public eye, living with her family in Michigan, Smith resumed her musical career in the 1990s. She spent the first decade of the twenty-first century writing what became *Just Kids*, a National Book Award–winning tour de force about her coming of age with Mapplethorpe. The book perfectly captured both the particular zephyr of downtown New York in the 1970s and something even more elusive and wonderful: the tender hearts of artists.

After Chicago native **LAURIE ANDERSON** (b. 1947) graduated from Barnard and completed an MFA in sculpture at Columbia University in 1972, she abandoned a gig teaching Egyptian and Assyrian architecture at City College in order to experiment with mixed-media installations and ephemeral, live-action art. One example of the latter: playing her violin while standing on a block of ice, wearing ice skates, performing until it melted.

While Anderson, who had begun playing the violin when she was eight, was interested primarily in the power of words and language, she was also fascinated by the power of technology, especially its ability to modify sound and visual imagery. Amid a residency at The Kitchen in SoHo, she composed several avant-garde performance pieces that combined musical work with visual and technological elements.

These led to widespread recognition in New York, which in turn led to invitations to perform in concert halls, art festivals, and museums abroad. But whereas many of her avant-garde peers eschewed mainstream outlets, infusing their work with haughty solemnity, Anderson, who grew up with seven siblings and has a gentle, elfin presence, was thrilled for her work to reach a broader public, once telling an interviewer she wanted to make things that "wouldn't just sit in museums."

In 1980, "O Superman"—her song exploring the intersection of humanity and technology with electronically altered speech—climbed the pop charts. It generated so much interest that Warner Bros. gave her a recording contract, the result of which was the 1982 release of *Big Science*, her first solo album.

Over the next three decades, Anderson starred in and directed her first film, experimented with various sound technologies, invented several new machines (including a bow for her violin made from recorded magnetic tape), and produced more spoken word albums and a CD-ROM. She also published eight books, created a multi-media presentation inspired by Herman Melville's *Moby Dick*, collaborated with other artists—including the choreographer Trisha Brown, the Paris Opera Ballet, and the singer and songwriter Lou Reed (her partner of nearly two decades)—and became NASA's first artist-in-residence.

By embracing rather than rejecting establishment venues, Anderson brought her vanguard work to large audiences, thereby breaking down barriers in the New York art scene. She also showed other artists how to remain true to their vision while nonetheless becoming a vital voice in speaking out against what David Bowie once called "the tyranny of the mainstream."

Nowhere was this more evident than in 2015, when she arranged for the live projection (or "telepresence") of Mohammed el Gharani, one of the youngest men detained by the United States at the Guantanamo prison, into the center of the cavernous Park Avenue Armory, where, amid a celestial-like light display and a soundscape derived from guitar reverb, visitors could reflect on time, space, and the human impact of American foreign policy.

THE INTELLECTS

By the time German-born philosopher **HANNAH ARENDT** (1906–1975) arrived in New York in 1941, she had already witnessed some of our species' ugliest behaviors, and had begun her intellectual inquiry into the complexities of the human condition.

A preternaturally bright child, Arendt lost her father when she was just seven, having watched him slowly overtaken by paresis, or syphilitic insanity. As a young adult, she studied with famed philosopher Martin Heidegger, then Karl Jaspers, who supervised her doctoral dissertation. She went on to work for a Zionist organization, but her efforts were halted in 1933 when she was arrested by the political police in Berlin.

After fleeing to Paris, she was rounded up with other Jews and sent by train to a detention camp in Gurs. She managed to escape, and with help from an American rescue committee, she made her way first to Portugal and from there to the Upper West Side.

Soon after arriving in New York, she became closely associated with the influential literary journal *Partisan Review*. Her major works, including the three-part *The Origins of Totalitarianism*, published in 1951, and *The Human Condition* in 1958, not only shaped the focus of inquiry among the City's intellectuals but also would eventually become essential political philosophy texts of the twentieth century. Meanwhile, her frequent essays in the City's most erudite publications—including *Commentary*, *Dissent*, and *The New York Review of Books*—put her at the center of the debate.

It was a five-part series in *The New Yorker* about a Nazi war criminal, however, that caused bitter divisions within the New York intellectual world, divisions so acute that social critic Irving Howe lamented two decades later that they "would never be entirely healed."

Sent by the magazine to observe the trial of Adolf Eichmann, a Nazi leader who had personally arranged for over 1.5 million Jews to be sent to killing centers, Arendt watched—as did much of the world—as the horrific nature of the Holocaust was described in chilling detail by the prosecutor, survivors, and Eichmann himself, who testified from behind bulletproof glass.

Yet Arendt didn't describe Eichmann in the way most people expected—as akin to the devil incarnate. Instead, she described him instead as a thoughtless bureaucrat who looked "terribly and terrifyingly normal." The label she gave to the conundrum of his "normalcy" and what he had done was "the banality of evil," a concept so beyond what most people took for common sense that she elicited near-universal outrage.

Compounding the proposal that "evil" could be something other than the deliberate machinations of a malevolent actor, Arendt also acknowledged, with her characteristic pragmatism, the role of some German Jewish leaders in aiding Nazi predators, which most German Jewish intellectuals and many others interpreted as tantamount to blaming the victim.

The uproar was swift and fierce. There were more than a thousand published responses, and a bitter public dispute emerged among intellectuals and others who disagreed with—or were offended by—her thesis. "Every intellectual in New York had to take sides," the head of the Hannah Arendt Center for Politics and Humanities at Bard College, Roger Berkowitz, told me. "No one was neutral. It was war."

This "war" became a scandal, and a defining moment in New York's intellectual life: as described by Howe, the founding editor of *Dissent*, in his comprehensive 1969 essay "The New York Intellectuals," the "violent dispute" showed that "[n]owhere else in the country could there have been the kind of public . . . debate sometimes ugly and outrageous, yet urgent and afire."

Arendt went on to teach at the Graduate Faculty of New School for Social Research, publish essays on American political life, and write two volumes of an uncompleted work, *The Life of the Mind*, which was published posthumously in 1978.

Today, the Hannah Arendt Center at Bard College, established exactly a century after her birth, promotes the cause which Arendt, the embodiment of a New York thinker, so passionately manifested. In her name, the school is committed to combatting the "absence of thinking—which is so ordinary an experience in our everyday life, where we have hardly the time, let alone the inclination, to stop and think."

This sensibility remains crucial—indeed our only hope—of overcoming hatred and other elements of totalitarianism, something Arendt spent her life trying to teach us.

After graduating from high school in Southern California at the age of fifteen, **SUSAN SONTAG** (1933–2004), a rapacious explorer of ideas, went on to earn two master's degrees and undertake doctoral work in philosophy. But it was during a trip to Paris in 1957 that she discovered an engaged intellectual community outside of academic institutions, something she would be instrumental in fostering in New York.

Upon returning to the States, she moved to the City in 1959 and resolved to become a writer. With an omnivorous appetite for literature, film, philosophy, art, and aesthetic movements of all kinds, no subject was too obscure or foreign for Sontag's critical attention, and she quickly found numerous outlets for her passionate, elegantly composed essays. By applying the tools of an academic to a vast array of cultural, political, and artistic developments, she made even the most esoteric of ideas comprehensible to a wide audience of readers, which helped bring about the kind of thoughtful, provocative conversations she had observed taking place in Paris.

In 1964 she published two particularly notable essays. "Notes on 'Camp,'" which appeared in *Partisan Review,* argued for the value of high and low culture; "Against Interpretation," printed in the *Evergreen Review,* chastised

highbrow critics for a bourgeois failure to allow the importance of art on its own merits. Both pieces so stirred New York's intelligentsia that she immediately attracted attention from all corners of the City.

LITERATURE IS FREEDOM.

—SUSAN SONTAG, 2003

Sontag was among the first contributors to *The New York Review of Books*. Over the years she would continue to publish there and in *The New Yorker* in between producing a steady stream of novels and essay collections for the eminent publishing house Farrar, Straus and Giroux. She also published in mainstream magazines like *Vogue, Mademoiselle, Harper's Bazaar, Life*, and *Time*, all of which put her name and ideas into popular circulation. Taken together, for four decades she worked to bridge the previously self-contained and insular world of the literary elite with the City's wider consciousness.

Some of her essays, like the book-length *On Photography*, became instant classics, posing essential, ingenious questions regarding how to engage with art or technology. Others, like the short story "The Way We Live Now," serve as definitive works in that they so acutely capture the atmosphere of a particular historical moment—in this case, the HIV/AIDS crisis in the 1980s.

Sontag devoted endless hours to cultivating New York's arts and letters scene, mentoring younger writers, giving talks at Town Hall, and moderating readings at the 92nd Street Y. She also served as president of PEN American Center from 1987 to 1989, during which time she thrust New York's literary community onto the international stage by speaking out against the fatwa issued by Ayatollah Khomeini, the Supreme Leader of Iran, calling for Salman Rushdie to be put to death for his book *The Satanic Verses.*

Soon after the devastating and deadly attack on the World Trade Center, she spoke out against the dominant narrative of American impermeability widely repeated in the press, writing in the September 24, 2001, issue of *The New Yorker* that: "In the matter of courage (a morally neutral virtue): whatever may be said of the perpetrators of Tuesday's slaughter, they were not cowards." She also questioned the unanimity among political leaders and media pundits in denying the complexities of American foreign policy.

While her words stung the fresh wounds of the City and invited outrage from tabloids that branded her a traitor, the overarching thesis of her statements—that a mature democracy requires more honest engagement by all parties—would ultimately be proven crucial. Today, more than a decade after her death in 2004, this belief remains vital, especially in light of former CIA employee Edward Snowden's 2013 revelations regarding the extent to which the United States spies on its own citizens.

THE LOUDMOUTHS

The idea that New Yorkers are loud and judgmental surely predates Del Lord's 1932 comedy film short, *The Loud Mouth*, about a guy from Brooklyn who unabashedly offers his opinions to strangers, which constantly gets him into trouble. But, in the second half of the twentieth century, the outspokenness of several New York women would foster the City's identity as a place where phoniness and ineptitude are not tolerated.

After seeing several cabaret shows while growing up in Detroit, Michigan, ELAINE STRITCH (1925–2014) became determined to live her life in the spotlight. So while still a teenager she moved to New York to follow her dream. Or, at least at first, it was her dream with a twist, since her strict Catholic parents required that she live in a convent. All the same, she took acting classes for about a year before she landed her first gig in a small off-Broadway show. Then, in 1946, she made her debut on the Great White Way.

Over a career that would span nearly seven decades, Stritch—whose hilarious, acerbic personality onstage was matched (or perhaps superseded) by her irascible personality offstage—would work with many of Broadway's leading lights. These included Noël Coward and Stephen Sondheim, who, for his 1970 musical *Company*, wrote "Ladies Who Lunch," Stritch's ultimate showcase: a biting, tragicomic skewering of rich socialites and their attendant difficulties that also revealed the intense blend of insecurity, jealousy, and anger her character—and, as it happens, she, too—felt underneath.

Offstage, Stritch was likewise hilarious and astringent, a tough broad with a whiskey voice whose wisecracks revealed a breathtaking mix of arrogance and vulnerability, including a forty-year battle with alcoholism.

In her seventh decade, Stritch took up residence in the posh Carlyle Hotel. She continued working well into her eighties, landing a recurring role on Tina Fey's *30 Rock* and costarring with Bernadette Peters in *A Little Night Music*. Her one-woman show directed by George C. Wolfe, *Elaine Stritch at Liberty*, won both a Tony and a Drama Desk Award.

In 2014, Stritch finally "left the building," her favorite and oft-employed euphemism for death. But her legacy as a bigmouth—and de facto truth-teller—endures. "Few people have been so honest about what it takes to be on a stage, or so direct about how much some people desire the spotlight, drink it in, and live off of it," Rachel Syme later wrote in *The New Yorker*. "If nothing else, she was relentlessly true."

Truth is something **JOAN RIVERS** (1933–2014), the Brooklyn-born daughter of Russian immigrants, was never afraid to confront, no matter how painful. In fact, it was at the heart of the abrasive and self-deprecating comedy she began practicing in the early 1960s, first in Greenwich Village coffeehouses, then in its comedy clubs; it was also what eventually made her the first female stand-up to succeed in the attack tradition—something that was extra challenging given what one prominent critic blithely described in 1965 as her "handicap" of being "a woman comic."

An appearance on *The Tonight Show Starring Johnny Carson* in 1965 ushered her into the big time. After this she served as Carson's backup as well as hosting several of her own shows, during which she coined her iconic catchphrase "Can we talk?" (This inquiry typically preceded a harsh and funny line, like when she asked a guest point-blank, "Who's your favorite husband?" before counting off their names on her fingers.)

In the early 1970s she worked around censors and dared to make jokes about sex, divorce, and abortion. When the singer Karen Carpenter died from anorexia in 1983, Rivers declared, "I refuse to feel sorry for anyone thin enough to be buried in pleats."

The ultimate showcase for Rivers's outrageous wit began in 1995 when she created and cohosted, with her daughter, Melissa, *Live from the Red Carpet* for the E! Entertainment Television network. Like a Jewish aunt whose neural inhibitors had malfunctioned, she sandbagged celebrities and demanded, "Who are you wearing?" before offering skewering comments to the cameras, like: "If Kate Winslet had dropped a few pounds, the *Titanic* would never have sunk."

But no one was more victimized by Rivers's stilettos than was Rivers herself. In a quest to stay young, she submitted repeatedly to plastic surgery, then mocked her own vanity: "I am definitely going to watch the Emmys this year! My makeup team is nominated for Best Special Effects."

She was also a successful author, QVC home shopping network host, and philanthropist; she often devoted her time and resources to God's Love We Deliver, a New York City charity created to deliver meals to those with HIV/AIDS. Rivers once explained her pioneering career this way: "I succeeded by saying what everyone else is thinking." After her unexpected death in 2014, the result of complications from yet another cosmetic surgery, the comedian Amy Schumer paid tribute: "I'm not going to say how big of balls she had . . . because she has taught us time and time again that having balls has nothing to do with it."

In the early 1970s one of the City's hottest nightclubs, the Continental, was actually a gay bathhouse that operated in the basement of the Ansonia hotel. There, a young performer, **BETTE MIDLER** (b. 1945)—accompanied by the pianist Barry Manilow, who frequently dressed, like the patrons, in only a white, waist-wrapped towel—let loose her inner diva, dazzling the nearly all-male crowd.

Two years later, with this devoted following firmly established, Midler turned her stage persona, The Divine Miss M, into the title of her first album; released by Atlantic Records in 1972, it contained many hit singles and achieved nationwide fame.

WHEN IT'S THREE O'CLOCK IN NEW YORK, IT'S STILL 1938 IN LONDON.

—BETTE MIDLER, 1978

Midler was an entertainment triple threat: blessed with powerful pipes, a capacity for great warmth in acting, and the ability to be funny. But it was saying things she's not supposed to—primarily speaking out for gay rights—that established her as one of the City's beloved bigmouths. For example, in 1973 she made a surprise appearance at a rally concluding one of the City's first gay pride parades. And in as early as 1975 she gave interviews to *The Advocate*, a prominent LGBTQ publication, and straightforwardly acknowledged her debt to the gay male audience.

During the first-ever Hollywood fundraiser in support of gay rights in 1977, Richard Pryor turned against the audience and declared, you all can "kiss my happy, rich black ass!" before walking off stage. Midler followed this by drolly asking, "Who wants to kiss this rich, white ass?"

In time, she began speaking out for the physical city itself. Midler grew up in Hawaii and has said she considers caring for the land to be as natural as breathing. In the mid-nineties, she was angered by what she considered the disgraceful mistreatment of NYC space in general, and of Fort Tryon Park in particular, a park in the uppermost portion of Manhattan that had been mired in trash and neglect for years. "I took one look and couldn't believe my eyes," Midler recalled to Marlo Thomas in 2012. "It was a dumping ground. People would come from all over the tri-state area and dump their trash. There was drug dealing and prostitution. I vividly remember people sitting at the bus stop outside the park, and the garbage was literally two feet high around them." So what did she do? She spent $300,000 of her own money, hired a crew of six, and cleaned up the park.

She also founded the New York Restoration Project (NYRP), which since 1995 has helped revitalize green spaces in the City's low-income neighborhoods, and began donating $2,000 a month to the City's Adopt-A-Highway trash pickup program, which led the City to post her name on the Bronx River Parkway. Then, when in 1999 the City announced a plan to auction off over a hundred neglected community gardens, Midler organized a coalition to save them; she then established a group to take ownership of sixty of them, as well as a volunteer program for their maintenance.

In 2003, Midler opened Sherman Creek Park on the Harlem River, which boasts Swindler Cove, a boathouse, a children's garden, and a facility where free environmental education programs are provided to poor students. The following year, she began paying to clean up two trash-polluted miles of the Major

Deegan Expressway near Yankee Stadium in the Bronx. By 2015, her New York Restoration Project had planted more than a million trees in the City.

Amidst her greening efforts, Midler all the while continued recording new albums and starring in shows. In 2015 she undertook her tenth international concert tour, Divine Intervention, to promote her latest album, *It's the Girls!*

In 2016, at age seventy, Midler shows no signs of slowing down—or keeping quiet. She is scheduled to star in a revival of *Hello, Dolly!* opening on Broadway in 2017. And just a few hours before the Oscars aired in February she sent a tweet out to her followers taking a position on the #OscarsSoWhite controversy: "The Oscars are today! You know, the awards show where Leonardo DiCaprio is 'overdue' but black people can 'wait till next year.'"

AFTER HOURS

Long before the mic drop meme entered popular culture, **MARY LOUISE CECELIA "TEXAS" GUINAN** (1884–1933), a spunky performer from Waco, Texas, picked up a microphone at a post-show party in 1924 and single-handedly transformed what had been a sedate soiree into a swinging, champagne-flowing bash.

Guinan had spent more than a decade trying to make it as an actress when Larry Fay, an enterprising bootlegger, observed her natural-born instinct for enticing reluctant sinners and promptly installed her as mistress of ceremonies at the El Fay, his soon-to-become legendary juice joint. Armed with a whistle, a booming voice, and a garish but loveable streak of sequins and wisecracks, Guinan perched on a stool in the center of the room, greeting visitors by shouting, "Hello, sucker!"—rendering guests willing and eager to part with their greenbacks.

Guinan's merriment-creating abilities led to the El Fay becoming one of the City's most popular speakeasies and Guinan being anointed queen of nightlife. Her reign continued even after she split with Fay and opened the 300 Club, which itself became a smash, making it a prime target for temperance-minded authorities. Several times in 1927 the club was padlocked and Guinan arrested, but each time she responded with characteristic aplomb, turning one nine-hour detention into an opportunity to entertain the precinct with her showgirls.

While anybody with a pulse and a dollar was welcome at Guinan's clubs, **RÉGINE ZYLBERBERG** (b. 1929) sought something different when she opened an American outpost of her namesake Parisian nightclub, Régine's, at the Delmonico Hotel in 1976. Charging a $600 membership fee, which guaranteed free entrance for clients with up to eight guests, Régine's offered the same mix of upscale clientele and elaborate, rotating theme parties that had drawn the likes of Brigitte Bardot and Premier Georges Pompidou to her original location. Indeed, droves of American A-listers flocked in, piqued by Régine's particular brand of charm (she was as likely to teach patrons the Hula-Hoop as the cha-cha), her never-ending flow of bubbly, and her hard-line stance about maintaining exclusivity.

"Texas" Guinan ring-led the Roaring Twenties. Régine invented bottle service and the velvet rope. And no one but the singer and model **GRACE JONES** (b. 1948) could crawl onto a stage several hours after midnight clad in nothing but Keith Haring's Maasai warrior–inspired body paint, blowing the minds of seventies revelers high on Quaaludes. After conquering Paris runways with her obsidian, statuesque beauty, Jones, a native of Jamaica raised in a Pentecostal family, returned to New York in the 1970s

BETTER A SQUARE
FOOT OF NEW YORK
THAN ALL THE REST OF
THE WORLD . . .
BETTER A LAMPPOST
ON BROADWAY THAN
THE BRIGHTEST STAR
IN THE SKY.

—TEXAS GUINAN, 1933

and found a fitting home in Studio 54 for what *The New York Times* called her "catwalk-Kabuki mischief and provocation." While pushing herself past every conceivable boundary, the sometimes singer, always provocateur performance artist became "The Disco Queen," forming alliances with a cadre of artists, producers, and fashion designers with whom she would eventually make films and record albums and produce other mayhem.

It was Jones's embrace of the outré that brought gender-bending, avant-garde exploration out of the art studios and into NYC nightlife, paving the way for later fantasyland-style nightclubs like The Roxy, Limelight, and the Palladium, where in the 1980s deejay Anita Sarko would bridge the City's punk and disco scenes and open new worlds of musical crossover.

GRACE JONES

THE GROCERS

The diets of the original residents of New York—the Lenape—had been flavorful and seasonally diverse. But after two centuries of Dutch and English rule, later residents developed more austere culinary habits; according to William Grimes's *Appetite City: A Culinary History of New York*, by the 1820s "local tastes ran to beef, beer, oysters, and bread." That began to change in the 1840s, when immigrants from other parts of Europe began expanding New Yorkers' palates with a wider variety of foods and spices, launching what would make New York for many years the most diverse culinary city in the world.

German émigrés hawked sausages and cabbage, often traveling with a shaver to slice the vegetable for making sauerkraut at home. Eastern Europeans sold pickles, pretzels, breads, and knishes. Italians purveyed peanuts, chestnuts, fruits, and vegetables, including dandelion greens, which they scavenged from empty lots on the Lower East Side. Indeed, members of nearly all ethnic groups vended, though their histories were unfortunately rarely recorded.

An exception: **LILLIAN HARRIS DEAN** (1870–1928), known as Pig Foot Mary, sold pigs' feet, hog maws, and chitterlings (or "chitlins") out of a repurposed baby carriage at the corner of West 135th Street—what is now Malcolm X Boulevard.

As their resources grew, some peddlers expanded by renting large wooden pushcarts, which could be had for ten cents a day in the 1880s. Others opened stalls in one of more than a dozen markets that existed in that era, including the Fulton, Jefferson, and Catharine Markets, as well as the Essex Street Market, which operated off Ludlow Street before moving to its current location at Delancey Street in 1940.

Women and children were as likely as men to operate as peddlers; the "hot corn girls" hawking cobs from cedar pails filled with hot water were as legendary in the nineteenth century as hot dog and pretzel cart vendors would become in the late twentieth. And though most of the grocers operating stalls in the markets were men, Thomas DeVoe, writing in *The Market Book* in 1862, noted how Elizabeth Kline petitioned the Catherine Market in 1801 for permission to sell coffee and chocolate, and a "Mrs. Jeroleman" sold hot coffee and doughnuts at the Oswego Market.

But it was in the twentieth century that several women helped establish specialty food stores with a lasting influence on the City.

One such store—and story—begins with a father named Joel Russ. After immigrating from Strzyzów, a rural village in what is now southern Poland, Russ had trod the streets peddling strings of mushrooms on his shoulders before switching to selling herring out of a barrel. He saved enough money for a pushcart, then a horse and wagon. In 1914, he opened his first store, J. Russ Cut Rate Appetizing, on Orchard Street; six years later he moved it around the corner to East Houston, where he broadened his inventory of pickled and cured fish.

In the store's tenth year, Joel's oldest daughter, **HATTIE RUSS GOLD** (1913–2014), just eleven years old herself, began working alongside her father. In time her sisters, **IDA RUSS SCHWARTZ** (1915–2001) and **ANNE RUSS FEDERMAN** (b. 1921), took their places behind the counter as well. Then, in 1933, their father made a business decision considered shocking at the time: he changed the name of his business to Russ & Daughters—an event that made the newspapers, since it was almost unheard of to name a business after daughters rather than sons. "Our delivery truck used to get stopped," Hattie Russ Gold recalled. "People wanted to know if that was really the name. They couldn't believe it."

Today, more than one hundred years after selling its first lox, Russ & Daughters is still family-run, and, as the Smithsonian Institute puts it, is a "part of New York's cultural heritage." That success is due largely to Federman, a tireless toiler who continued to oversee the store with her husband, Herb, even after Schwartz left in the forties and Gold left in the sixties. Even after the Federmans' son, Mark, joined the business in the late seventies with his wife, Maria, Federman remained the matriarch and guiding spirit. In 2009, Mark and Maria passed the torch to their daughter, Niki Russ Federman, a fourth generation owner, who, today, runs the business with Joshua Russ Tupper, another one of Anne Russ Federman's grandchildren. In 2014, the pair of fourth generation owners opened the company's first restaurant, Russ & Daughters Cafe, two and a half blocks away; this was followed by a bakery and a second sit-down eatery inside the Jewish Museum on the Upper East Side.

As a young woman, **LILLIAN ZABAR** (1905–1995) fled the pogroms of her homeland and traveled alone to the United States, where she lived with relatives in Philadelphia and worked as a hatmaker. On a visit to New York, she ran into an acquaintance from her Ukrainian village, Louis Zabar, and in 1927 they married.

Louis, an illegal immigrant who had entered the States via Canada, had no papers—and therefore had no work option but self-employment. So the couple worked in a deli in the Brighton Beach area of Brooklyn, then sold produce on Flatbush Avenue.

In 1934, believing they could earn a better living on the Upper West Side of Manhattan, then an affluent Jewish neighborhood, Lillian and Louis opened a smoked fish counter in a bustling market on Broadway. By 1941 they were successful enough to move into another Broadway storefront between 80th and 81st Streets, where they introduced some of the prepared foods Lillian had grown up with: blintzes, potato salad, stuffed cabbage, and coleslaw.

Over the years, the store expanded to fill several additional storefronts on the block and added a wider variety of products. Today, Zabar's continues to be a beacon of Eastern European specialties. Saul Zabar, one of the couple's three sons, who has been running the store with his brother Stanley since about 1960, told me that today their store sells in excess of 1,000 pounds of smoked salmon every week.

In 1946, **MARIA BALDUCCI** (1900–1989) and her husband, Louis, opened a fruit stand at the triangle-shaped intersection at Christopher Street and Greenwich Avenue. Before sunrise every morning, Louis visited wholesalers and acquired the day's inventory; upon his return, he'd nap while Maria manned the outfit—which was essentially a shack. Soon they developed a reputation for selling off-season produce, a nearly unheard-of practice in the mid-twentieth century, which earned them business from many of the City's prominent restaurants, including Lüchow's.

In 1972, when the couple had to vacate their spot, they decided to move into an empty storefront across Sixth Avenue at 9th Street—but as it was 3,000 square feet, they needed to fill the space. Louis had for years been bringing home produce too blemished to sell, with which Maria made Italian specialties for their family. It was an obvious next step to try selling them in the store.

"She started bringing roasted peppers, fried peppers, stuffed eggplant—and it would sell in a blink of an eye," her daughter Grace Balducci Doria told me. A kitchen was built in the cellar, from which emerged an endless parade of Italian fare like steaming stuffed artichokes, hearty lasagna, and braciole, or grilled, rolled-up flank steak stuffed with cheese and breadcrumbs, creating aromas that stopped shoppers in their tracks and lured them to the counter.

Many of the City's food writers excitedly chronicled the store's new introductions: like the arrival of spaghetti squash in 1978, or fresh pasta in 1980. Over time, as New Yorkers' palates expanded, so too did their requests for ever more exotic products, leading Balducci's to become an early purveyor of imported oils, vinegars, and other (then) hard-to-find condiments. Today, there are six supermarkets and two "gourmet on the go" stores using the Balducci's name, including one inside the Hearst Building.

In 1898, a Lebanese immigrant named Abrahim Sahadi opened a store on Washington Street in Little Syria, a neighborhood south and west of the World Trade Center site, where he sold imported lentils, pistachios, and olives. In the 1920s, he hired on his nephew Wade. Two decades later, when construction began on a tunnel connecting their neighborhood to Brooklyn, Wade purchased a building on Brooklyn's Atlantic Avenue; under the stewardship of his sons, Charlie and Robert, that store would continue to provide Middle Eastern foodstuffs for half a century.

But it was Charlie's daughter, the fourth-generation family member **CHRISTINE SAHADI WHELAN** (b. 1966), who concluded that the store's ethnically diverse customers would enjoy prepared Middle Eastern specialties. In 1986, Whelan, a culinary-school-trained food-lover, added a prepared foods department to the market from which she sold humus, kibbee, and lebany. These she prepared using recipes from her mother, Audrey Sahadi, a native of Aleppo, Syria—with input from hired cooks of Persian and Egyptian descent. Sahadi's prepared foods counter soon became an important lunch-time destination for the legions of workers in downtown Brooklyn. And as a reliable source of takeout and catering, it also helped to fuel the borough's ever-widening obsession with all things gastronomic.

Throughout the nineties and into the twenty-first century, Whelan would continue to add an ever-wider array of specialty foods from around the world—even from regions facing political conflict. Owing to the family's long-standing relationships with farmers and spice purveyors in Lebanon and Syria, the store continued to supply the City's home cooks and professional chefs with products that would otherwise be hard to come by.

In early 2016, at age seventy-two, Charlie, a gregarious and beloved fixture in the neighborhood, decided to "retire"; for him this means working in the store just one or two days a week instead of six. Aided by her Uncle Bob and her brother Ron, Whelan remains at the helm of the store five days a week, where she champions the renaissance of artisanal foodstuffs lately embraced by young Brooklynites.

THE RESTAURATEURS

Over the twentieth century, several women had a hand in creating a restaurant scene that, today, is a central draw of City life. But in the nineteenth century, the social hubs of New York life were taverns where men—and almost never women—convened around beverages; food was a secondary consideration.

That became a bit of a problem in the 1890s, when women began joining the office workforce in great numbers. Existing establishments that sold prepared food were typically steakhouses or pubs that offered greasy, gut-pleasing heavy fare more suited to men. (Even today, the menu at McSorley's Old Ale House, one of the oldest Irish bars in the City, consists of little more than a liverwurst sandwich, a burger, or a plate of cheese and crackers with onions.) Saloonkeepers didn't know what to do about the sudden influx of skirt-wearing patrons—but Jane Shattuck did.

In 1898, candy salesman Frank Shattuck opened a store at Broadway and 36th Street to sell chocolates made by the Boston company Schrafft's. Soon afterward his sister, **JANE SHATTUCK** (1865–1948), thought to add a menu of tea-room fare: light sandwiches—including grilled cheese and "fresh asparagus on toast"—salads, and ice cream sodas, all offered in a bright, dainty setting well suited to this new type of working woman.

With this innovation, one of the City's most legendary restaurant chains was born, and the dames showed up in droves. By 1928, the revenue at Schrafft's restaurants from lunch was $1 million a month; before long, 18 outlets dotted the City. Frank M. Shattuck, a great-grandson of the founder, told me that one house specialty in particular contributed to the restaurant's popularity: whiskey. "Women would sip gin and whiskey out of their dainty little tea cups. Very discreet," he shared. "They made the whiskey in-house. It was a well-kept secret."

With its many locations, the ubiquity of Schrafft's—combined with its genteel atmosphere and pleasing menu—helped to overturn the previously long-standing stigma about women being seen having a meal in public. All told, Schrafft's was one of several attractive restaurants that gave rise to NYC being seen as an attractive dining destination.

Even as recently as the sixties, most Americans still regarded Italian fare as exotic, and knew of only Southern Italian red sauce dishes. These were publicly introduced, in part, by **LUISA LEONE** (1870–1940).

Leone often hosted large dinner parties for the friends and clients of her wine merchant husband. It was at one such gathering that the Italian tenor Enrico Caruso commented that Luisa's cooking deserved a wider showing; he then talked her skeptical husband into granting permission for her to open a restaurant. So, in 1906 she unveiled Leone's, inside their home on West 34th

Street. On opening night, which included Caruso, they could fit just twenty diners at a time, and the seven-course meal she offered was priced at fifty cents.

The restaurant, an instant hit, expanded over the years, eventually occupying eleven dining rooms over 35,000 square feet on 48th Street. In 1959, it was acquired by Restaurant Associates, who changed its name to Mama Leone in tribute to its founder. (By then the quality of the food was rather lackluster, nothing like during the restaurant's heyday.) According to William Grimes in *Appetite City: A Culinary History of New York*, the $4 million in profits Mama Leone's brought in helped then-nascent Restaurant Associates bankroll some of the City's most famed dining establishments, including the Four Seasons and Central Park's Tavern on the Green. Joe Baum, Restaurant Associates's original president, would later go on to open many more legendary fine dining spots, like Windows on the World, with the help of pioneering City foodies like Barbara Kafka and Rozanne Gold.

EDNA LEWIS (1916–2006) grew up in Freetown, a close-knit community in Virginia where her family lived off the land and prepared food according to the seasons. Later living in New York, she was known among friends for hosting convivial dinner parties with delicious food. So, when in 1948 her friend Johnny Nicholson planned to open a café in the rear garden of his antique store on East 58th Street, she easily talked him into letting her oversee its fare. A week later, Lewis was running Café Nicholson, a fanciful spot that quickly charmed the City's artsy and intellectual types.

At this time, NYC already had plenty of what Grimes described to me as "snooty French restaurants and he-man steakhouses," whereas Lewis was among the first to serve truly delectable dishes in a quirky and relaxed setting. Café Nicholson was something of a shared secret among the in-crowd; devotees included Truman Capote, Paul Robeson, Eleanor Roosevelt, Gore Vidal, and Tennessee Williams.

In the mid-fifties, Lewis left the restaurant (which had by then moved to a larger space), instead embarking on other adventures, including authoring important cookbooks documenting American food history—rightfully the primary source of her acclaim. Still, Lewis's concept of a restaurant—bringing inquisitive people together over flawless, satisfying food in an unexpected setting—was an important forerunner to many distinctive restaurants later opened by women in the City. These included Buonavia, opened in 1971 by Lidia Bastianich in the Forest Hills section of Queens, the namesake regional Mexican restaurant started in 1987 by Zarela Martinez in Midtown, and Prune, opened in 1999 by Gabrielle Hamilton in the East Village.

A decade and a half after Lewis introduced her carefully prepared American dishes to the City, another Southern-born chef, SYLVIA WOODS (1926–2012), opened an eponymous luncheonette that for decades reigned as Harlem's de facto social center. Sylvia's Restaurant opened in 1962 at Lenox Avenue near 127th Street, offering fried chicken, ribs, corn bread, and hot cakes.

With six booths and fifteen stools, it wasn't large, but the immense popularity of the food drew local and national politicians, celebrities, and food lovers from all over the City. The Queen of Soul Food eventually acquired more space and Sylvia's became the cornerstone for more commercial development in Harlem. Arthur Schwartz, the NYC restaurant expert and Food Maven podcaster, also credits Woods with helping break down color barriers between white and black residents. "In the old days," he told me, "Sylvia's was the only place where white people could go to and feel comfortable in Harlem. After church all the church ladies would go to Sylvia's. The politicians would go to Sylvia's. So you always heard about Sylvia's and it made you feel safe. Sylvia's was very welcoming to everybody."

THE TASTEMAKERS

Long before competitive cooking shows, online restaurant reservations, and food truck festivals, a small handful of epicures were among the country's first exponents of gastronomy, avidly championing the pleasures of eating well.

For example, the food section of *The New York Times* had long included only tips for homemakers; it wasn't until the 1960s that Craig Claiborne began broadening their coverage, bringing in food criticism and creating the four-star rating system. And even when MIMI SHERATON (b. 1926) succeeded Claiborne as the *Times*'s restaurant critic in 1975—assuming the post after a twenty-year career as a freelance food writer—dining out was still not a regular part of American life.

Having grown up in a food-loving Brooklyn family, Sheraton delighted in all things gastronomic; similarly, she served more than eight years at the paper as her many readers' gastronomic guide. In search of the City's best chicken salad, she over time sampled sixty kinds from thirty-one shops. With the aim of deciphering Thai food for the uninitiated, she explained in 1978 how it "combines elements of the Chinese, Malaysian, and Indian kitchens." She also helped natives and visitors alike figure out where to eat, so as not to miss, as she advised in 1976, "some of the best atmosphere and most interesting food in the country."

WE HAVE HIGHER QUALITY CONVERSATIONS IN RESTAURANTS THAN AT HOME. IT'S AS THOUGH WE RISE TO THE OCCASION BY SELECTING WORTHWHILE, LESS MUNDANE SUBJECTS TO DISCUSS WHEN EATING OUT.

—MIMI SHERATON, 2004

Sheraton—who over the course of eleven months tasted all 1,196 items in the Bloomingdale's food department for an article in *New York* magazine—patiently helped readers "who might not have had time, money or, most importantly, the interest and natural inclination to learn the finer points of eating," explaining foods, describing restaurant practices, and demystifying unknown cuisines.

Sheraton also became known for her frank, unvarnished delivery of a restaurant's failings. In 1978, she complained about a bistro's "tendency to garnish luncheon dishes drugstore-style, with a wedge of unripe tomato and a limp lettuce leaf." A review in 1983 warned readers: "As a rule of thumb, avoid anything made with a cream or near-cream sauce."

Later, she penned an award-winning *Vanity Fair* article about the fortieth anniversary of the Four Seasons hotel and restaurant, in addition to about a dozen books, including *1,000 Foods to Eat Before You Die*. In the days before the word "foodie" even existed, Sheraton taught New Yorkers just what it meant to be one.

Another important herald of the City's restaurant scene was **GAEL GREENE** (b. 1933), a freelance writer for *McCall's* and *Cosmopolitan* who became the nascent *New York* magazine's first restaurant reviewer.

Greene, a native of Detroit and self-described sybarite, threw herself into the role, gleefully recounting every last morsel she consumed in the City's best restaurants.

Like her counterparts in the New Journalism movement of the sixties, Greene, whose hunger for sex is as notorious as her appetite for food, worked in the first person, using lusty language to build passionate, sometimes shocking crescendos of satisfaction.

Writing in 1969, here's how she described meals at Café Chauveron:

GREAT SENSUOUS FEASTS TO STAGGER HOME FROM, GIGGLING, PLEASED WITH THE SHEER BRILLIANCE OF HAVING CHOSEN SO WELL. LES MOULES AU CHABLIS GLACÉES, MUSSELS BURIED IN A SUBLIME WINE SAUCE ENRICHED WITH WHIPPED CREAM, THEN GLAZED UNDER THE SALAMANDER. TENDER, PINK-FLESHED RACK OF LAMB WITH PRIMEURS, INFANT VEGETABLES TASTING AS IF THEY'D BEEN GROWN IN BUTTER. AND THEN A GREAT VOLUPTUOUSNESS OF THE CHOCOLATE, THE CHAUVE-RON MOUSSE—THE SOPHIA LOREN OF MOUSSES—GUTSY, NOT THE LEAST BIT SUBTLE, WRAPPED IN A THIN SPONGE-CAKE PACKAGE, SERVED WITH A WHIPPED-CREAM-FLUFFED SABAY-ON SAUCE AND—HOLY GLUTTONY!—MOIST ALMOND-SCENTED MACAROONS. FRESH STRONG CAFÉ FILTRE. MEASURE THAT CLIMAX, DR. MASTERS!

Buoyed by both the adventurous spirit of the 1960s and early 1970s and her editors' desire to publish a brash reflection of the City, Greene helped legitimize the idea of dining out as a form of entertainment. And after half a century of relentless pleasure-hunting—her thirty-four-year run as critic was followed by her Ask Gael column, which she still writes at age eighty three—she has proven herself to be truly insatiable, which became the title of her 2006 autobiography.

In 1993, **RUTH REICHL** (b. 1948), who grew up in Greenwich Village but spent her formative years immersed in California's food revolution, returned to New York from the West Coast, bringing with her all the talents developed over her time as a chef, restaurant owner, and food writer and critic, including for the *Los Angeles Times*.

Donning elaborate disguises so as to not be recognized as a critic, she infiltrated the City's fine dining temples—then smartly demystified them for readers, explaining ever-more complex dishes and cutting through the haughty façade many eateries presented. She also treated ethnic food with the same respect accorded fine French technique—something earlier writers, in their zeal to celebrate the arrival of sophisticated cooking, had overlooked. (Beginning in 2012, this approach would be elevated anew by the *Times*'s Ligaya Mishan who does for unsung ethnic restaurants in her weekly column, Hungry City, what Lester Bangs did for rock.)

Reichl's time in the critic's perch overlapped directly with an explosion in the NYC restaurant culture—brought on, in part, from the opening of Jams in

1984 and the expansion of big-money restaurant-as-spectacle palaces. For more than four decades, writing for the *Times* as well as authoring her own books, she has served as an important guardian of food as a central, authentic expression of love. In 1999, Reichl left her critic's post to be *Gourmet* magazine's editor-in-chief, where she would do even more to awaken the national consciousness to the deeper importance of food.

In 1979, **NINA ZAGAT** (b. 1942) and her husband Tim, both lawyers who enjoyed dining out, were at a dinner party when one of the guests complained that restaurant reviews at a major newspaper had been unreliable.

Tim suggested they survey their friends for their own restaurant reviews; before long, the couple had compiled the opinions of two hundred friends and associates reviewing one hundred NYC restaurants. They printed out the results on legal paper and shared them with friends, who found their makeshift guide surprisingly handy for picking just the right spot for clients. Whereas professional critics use literary finesse to celebrate the finer points of gastronomy and décor, what was particularly helpful about these amateur reviews was that ordinary diners provided useful firsthand tips on practical concerns, like cost, waiting times, and service.

Inspired by the response, the Zagats (pronounced zah-GAT as in "the cat") pitched their idea for a crowd-sourced guide to several publishers—who turned them down, "claiming local content would never sell." "The fact that our vision was to have something that was social, local, and mobile was the reason that the professionals rejected us," Nina Zagat told an alumni publication for her alma mater, Vassar, in 2013. But, "Of course, that's exactly the reason the guides became popular."

Soon, the couple began self-publishing, driving boxes of books to New York bookstores. After a cover story about the guide in *New York* magazine in 1986, sales took off, quickly reaching 75,000 per month. By the 1990s—before the Internet became central to American life—the guide functioned as a bible for the growing cult of food-obsessed New Yorkers, who often worked their way through the list of top-rated restaurants to ensure they had experienced all the best offerings in the City.

"We would give people a way to make smart decisions for themselves about what was most important to them on a particular day," Zagat told me, referring to the practice of separately rating the categories for food, décor, and service. "People are looking for different things at different times; we empowered them to make their own decisions for a particular occasion."

The arrival of the Internet meant that the Zagat guide competed with an infusion of crowd-sourced eating guides in the form of Yelp. But that doesn't take away the fact that, for years, the Zagat guide served as the primary directory for a devoted foodie's explorations. Plus, it's now available for readers both in and beyond the City, at www.zagat.com.

THE IN-CROWD

After restaurateur **ELAINE KAUFMAN** (1929–2010) opened her namesake bar and grill in 1963, she couldn't help but fuss over the struggling writers and artists who came in, encouraging them with kind words, free meals, and the occasional kick in the butt.

As the years passed and some of those young creatives bloomed into Woody Allen, Nora Ephron, George Plimpton and Gay Talese, and as a friend in public relations began bringing in more actors, agents, and directors, Elaine's soon became the preeminent clubhouse for the City's glitterati.

One reason Kurt Vonnegut Jr., Elaine Stritch, Lucille Ball, and George Steinbrenner, as well as Leonard Bernstein and Noel Coward, were all regulars at Elaine's was that Kaufman, heavyset and with an imposing presence, made the chosen ones feel at home, joining them at their tables, making introductions, and framing and hanging the authors' book covers. She also vociferously protected celebrated actors from wannabes and paparazzi—famously turning away anyone she didn't consider important enough to deserve a table along "the line" in the main dining room—and occasionally delivering rude rejoinders when those she considered unworthy (or, heaven forbid, a tourist) dared to question her treatment of them.

Whereas appearing impressed by celebrities was long considered a sign of unsophistication, Elaine Kaufman mastered the art of nonchalance. In response to a visitor asking how to get to the powder room, she once replied, "Take a right at Michael Caine."

Her establishment was so well known—and so quintessentially New York—it had cameo roles in Woody Allen's 1979 film *Manhattan*, in the opening credits of *Saturday Night Live*, and in Billy Joel's song "Big Shot."

After she died from complications of emphysema in 2010, an heir had no choice but to close up shop, explaining, "There's no Elaine's without Elaine."

Long before Sardi's restaurant became a legendary Broadway institution, sixteen-year-old Eugenia Pallera, the eldest of six children from a poor northern Italian family, sailed alone to New York. She found work at the Bertholdi Inn, a boarding house in the theater district, where she met Vincent Sardi, another Piedmontese immigrant who had also found work at the Bertholdi. They married, and in 1921, they opened a small restaurant called "The Little Place" in an old brownstone on West 44th Street. Six years later, when the brownstone was torn down to build the St. James Theater, the couple moved their eatery to a new location down the block and rechristened it "Sardi's."

ELAINE KAUFMAN

Despite the apostrophe's misplacement, both Eugenia, by then known as **JENNY SARDI** (1889–1978), and her husband together created a clubhouse where the leading lights of Broadway's golden era, from playwright Tennessee Williams to the actors Helen Hayes and John Barrymore, would come to celebrate opening nights, await the first newspaper reviews, and—when gigs and money ran dry—seek comfort and camaraderie.

By the forties, Sardi's was the place to see and be seen, especially for aspiring stars—and the business folks who hoped to profit from them. In 1947, producer Brock Pemberton was lunching at Sardi's and lamenting the recent death of his business partner, Antoinette Perry, when he hatched the idea of establishing a theater prize in her memory. The prize was named the "Tony" Award, after Antoinette's nickname.

Thespians had been initially drawn to Sardi's not only for its central location but also because the couple had offered two menus: one for regular customers and another lower-priced "actor's menu." While Vincent was often publicly recognized for his generosity, which included feeding down-on-their-luck actors in exchange for IOUs (in 1947, the couple's son discovered a drawer with 500 or more of them dating back to the restaurant's opening), Jenny, a stunning brunette with a screen-siren figure, exuded a rare warmth that, along with the red leather banquettes and walls adorned with caricatures, was an intrinsic part of Sardi's magnetism.

In a biography about Lorenz Hart, half of the famous Broadway songwriting team Rodgers and Hart, Vincent Sardi described how Jenny tried to help the lyricist with his ongoing struggle with depression and alcoholism: "My wife Jenny treated him like a son," he said. "Unfortunately, he did not have much willpower. He would promise my wife that he was going to stop drinking so much, and then friends of his would arrive and ask him to sit down, and the next thing he knew he would be drinking again. Some nights when he would fall asleep, exhausted, my wife would make a bed for him in the back of the restaurant."

Jenny provided something else that was essential to Sardi's success, especially in its early days: hard work. From stocking the kitchen to cooking the food and functioning as a waitress and cashier, it was Jenny who kept the back of the house functioning. "She was basically the backbone of the operation," the current owner, Max Klimavicius, told me.

Indeed, Jenny was such a workhorse that when she finally retired in 1947, her son, Vincent Sardi Jr., who ran the business until his death in 2007, faced a quandary: "I had to hire three men to replace her, and they weren't her equal on the job," he told the Associated Press. In tribute, the restaurant now boasts a Eugenia Room, where special events like the Outer Critics Circle Awards are held.

THE AUNTIES

In the 1820s, two hundred years after Dutch settlers arrived on the island that natives called "Manahatta" (which meant "the place where we get bows"), a first great wave of European immigrants arrived from Ireland and Germany. A second wave from southern and eastern countries began around 1880. But after immigration laws changed in 1965, most new immigrants came from Latin America and Asia, a trend that continued well into the twenty-first century.

The arrival in New York of Dominicans, Puerto Ricans, Mexicans, Vietnamese, Indians, Thai, Sengalese, and many more ethnicities infused the medley of City life with even more rhythms and flavors. But it took some special women to help their *paesans* (or *bori* or *desi*) feel more at home in New York—while also protecting and celebrating cherished cultural traditions from back home.

In 1950, twenty-six-year-old **BETTY LEE SUNG** (b. 1924), a daughter of Chinese laundry owners, was hired to write scripts for the New York office of Voice of America. There she quickly became annoyed by the dearth of available information about Chinese contributions to American life. Even worse, the few published articles she could find in libraries were both inaccurate and overwhelmingly negative. As Sung later wrote in her autobiography, *Defiant Second Daughter: My First 90 Years*, "I mostly found reports that reinforced stereotypes of the Chinese as cheap laborers, opium smokers, undesirable heathens, and unassimilable aliens—ad nauseam."

Vowing to make known what she saw as the "intelligence, industry, and dignity" of New York's Chinese American community, Sung began attending male-only meetings of Chinatown's unofficial governing body—the Chinese Consolidated Benevolent Association—where she learned all about the activities in Chinatown. Then she gathered original source material from all over the country and in 1967 published her findings in her first book, *Mountain of Gold: The Story of the Chinese in America*; it was received with great acclaim, especially in academia, where Asian Americans had also previously been overlooked. As a result Sung was invited to create and teach one of the country's first classes about Asians at the City University of New York (CUNY), which was itself just opening to a more diverse population.

Soon after, with Sung's support, students successfully pressured CUNY into creating the country's first Asian Studies department. Sung was its first teacher; after continuing her research, earning a PhD, and publishing several more books, she became the department head.

She also cofounded the CUNY Asian American/Asian Research Institute and participated in dozens of conferences, seminars, and panels throughout the City. Though New York's Chinatown had existed since the 1880s, it was Sung who championed the work of Chinese immigrants, making its laborers, restaurants, and customs visible to the broader city.

Like Sung, ANTONIA PANTOJA (1922–2002), who was born in Puerto Rico and moved to New York in 1944, was troubled by the absence of her *compatriotas* in New York's public life—as well as by the crippling poverty of fellow immigrants in the barrios of the Bronx and Manhattan.

Utilizing both her training as a teacher and what acquaintances described as a powerful speaking voice, Pantoja undertook what became a decades-long career in community organizing and improving education for Nuyoricans. A few years after helping found New York's first Puerto Rican foster care and adoption agency in 1953, she helped create the Puerto Rican Forum, a broad-ranging advocacy group modeled on the NAACP and the American Jewish Committee. Then, in 1961 she established ASPIRA, an organization devoted to fostering education and leadership among Hispanic youth—which eventually won a landmark lawsuit forcing New York City to provide bilingual instruction.

ASPIRA, which means "inspire" in Spanish, was so successful in the Bronx that it grew into a national organization. But Pantoja, a tireless worker, didn't stop there: she also assisted Mayor John Lindsay with reforming the City's education system and helped forge a lasting toehold for Puerto Ricans in higher education by creating the institution that eventually became Boricua College.

Whereas many Puerto Ricans settled in the Bronx, immigrants from India often settled in Queens, which is where **DR. UMA MYSOREKAR** (b. 1944) landed in 1970. Making a home in Flushing, she observed how fellow Hindus lacked community resources and places to worship. So she joined with other Indians to establish the Hindu Temple Society of North America; and, in 1977, she helped consecrate the first Hindu place of worship in the country, on land previously used by a Russian Orthodox Church.

As Flushing became home to huge numbers of Chinese and Korean immigrants, Mysorekar resolved to make the Ganesh Temple, as the Hindu Temple Society of North America is commonly known (named for a Hindu deity), a resource for all her neighbors, Hindu and non-Hindu alike. She hosted celebrations for Diwali and other festivals and invited New Yorkers of all persuasions; she organized interfaith dialogues, reaching out to City Christians, Buddhists, and Jews; and, after relentless fund-raising, she opened a much-needed senior center, providing a place to go for the neighborhood's many elders.

Over the years, despite running a busy OB/GYN practice, Mysorekar gave increasingly more time to the temple. In 1989 she became a Society trustee; in 1994, she was elected president, at which point she began fund-raising for an expansion of the overcrowded facility in Flushing, which has become one of the most ethnically diverse areas in the country. Due largely to Mysorekar's efforts, and a personal donation of more than $1 million, the

DR. UMA MYSOREKAR

sixteen-thousand-square-foot community center opened in 1998, where it remains a beacon for city-dwellers and visitors from all over the world.

Whereas Mysorekar noticed how Hindus were largely absent from the public eye, **DEBBIE ALMONTASER** (b. 1966), a public schoolteacher who came from Yemen at the age of three, watched with dismay when, following the September 11 attacks, Arab Americans in New York City were subjected to unprecedented negative public scrutiny.

Having already been involved in Brooklyn's The Dialogue Project, a group of Jews, Palestinians, Muslims, Christians, and others who meet monthly to talk about the issues of the world, Almontaser recognized the need for New Yorkers to learn about the rich heritage of Arabs and Muslims. So she worked with Educators for Social Responsibility/Metro and Columbia University's Muslim Communities Project to develop curricula about Muslim and Arab history. She also cofounded the Brooklyn Bridges Project, a program through which members of the community can serve as escorts for women wearing religious garb who feel fearful about traveling around Brooklyn.

In 2005, Almontaser was asked to help found a school that became the Khalil Gibran International Academy (named after the Christian poet Khalil Gibran), the country's first English-Arabic public school. Unfortunately, in 2007, the *New York Post* incorrectly quoted her about a T-shirt—which read INTIFADA NYC;

created by a girls' youth group, the phrase referred not to the armed revolt of Palestinians against Israeli occupation, but to the word's literal meaning of "shaking off." In the ensuing media firestorm she was ousted from the school, although a federal court eventually found she was wrongfully terminated.

Since 2009 Almontaser has served as president of the board of directors of the Muslim Community Network, which organizes an array of programs to support New York's Muslim community, help parents and teachers of all backgrounds prevent bullying, and facilitate interfaith dialogue. It also puts on a conference for girls called "BElieve in YOUrself," through which, hopefully, the next generation of the City's leaders will learn from Almontaser's hard work and tenacity.

THE USHERS

After her opening night singing the lead role of Pamira in *L'Assedio di Corinto* at Teatro alla Scala in Milan in 1969, coloratura soprano **BEVERLY SILLS** (1929–2007) was nicknamed "La Fenomena" by the local press. Stateside, she was just as popular, having performed on radio and television to the delight of audiences in New York and beyond.

But it was in her second career as an arts administrator and advocate, which she began at age fifty in 1979, that America's Queen of Opera would make over the City's cultural life. After attending her first board meeting of New York City Opera in 1977, Sills, who was born in Brooklyn and known since childhood by the nickname "Bubbles," used her celebrity as a performer to raise more than a million dollars for the struggling organization. But when she became director in 1979, she learned the organization was several million dollars in debt. Though most judged the problems insurmountable, Sills refused to declare bankruptcy and instead relentlessly raised funds, no matter how dispiriting the process.

"There were days when I could hardly talk myself into coming to the office," Sills later told *Time* magazine. "There would be a big meeting on Tuesday morning, and I would be told there was no money for the Friday payroll."

But within five years finances were under control, at which point she ushered in a new era for the company, complete with an adventurous new repertory. In 1983 she made City Opera the first American opera house to introduce supertitles—translations projected above the stage during performances. Although they were enormously controversial at the time, they helped popularize the art form and were eventually adopted by nearly every opera company in the world.

In 1994 she became chair of the Lincoln Center for Performing Arts, the largest performing arts complex in the country. Over an eight-year term in the unpaid but enormously influential post, she introduced the annual Lincoln Center Festival, and hosted numerous "Live from Lincoln Center" television broadcasts. Wanting to ensure the center's longtime survival, she formed a committee to study the campus's brick-and-mortar needs. This became a $1.2 billion capital campaign that ultimately transformed the iconic campus—and put the organization on a stable course for the twenty-first century.

In her final act of stewardship, Sills assumed the title of chair of the Metropolitan Opera in 2002, where she had served on the board in a volunteer position since 1991. In addition to guiding the then-119-year-old company through the massive campus redevelopment, she convinced the board to install Peter Gelb as general manager. Then, after a longtime corporate sponsor withdrew support for Met Opera's Saturday afternoon radio broadcasts—which reach eleven million people in forty-two countries—she personally took to the airwaves to ask for support. She got it, and thanks to Sills, the broadcasts continue and the Met Opera endures.

IF I WAS AN OVER-
NIGHT'S SENSATION,
IT WAS CERTAINLY
THE LONGEST NIGHT'S
JOURNEY UNTO DAY
THAT ANYONE HAS
EVER SEEN.

—BEVERLY SILLS, 1976

In 1979, when **KAREN BROOKS HOPKINS** (b. 1951) became a fund-raiser for the Brooklyn Academy of Music, known as BAM, the notion of a Brooklyn-based cultural polestar was a tough sell.

Its Fort Greene location, a neighborhood first settled by black shipyard workers in the late nineteenth century, was a garbage-strewn eyesore, still mired in the economic depression and easy heroin of the 1970s. And the BAM's stately Beaux-Arts building, owned by the City, was badly in need of repair even before a thirty-inch water main burst under the adjacent street.

To add to the challenge, Manhattanites haughtily dismissed the idea of traveling to an outer borough—even though BAM is a mere four subway stops from Wall Street. "I would tell people a show would be at BAM and then in London, and people would say, 'okay, I'll see it in London,'" Hopkins told me. "They wouldn't want to cross that bridge."

But Hopkins, appreciating the institution's storied history, which stretched back before even the Civil War, saw through these trifles. And she saw the value in producing a venue for performers like Twyla Tharp and The Living Theatre. Over a thirty-five-year career, she has helped build BAM into both a world-class cultural establishment and the City's primary vehicle for reliable avant-garde and international programming.

Through relentless cheerleading, cajoling, and fund-raising, Hopkins—working for two decades with former president Harvey Lichtenstein—secured the funds to introduce in 1981 what became the Next Wave Festival, a program that looked beyond the established genres of theater and dance to highlight experimental and cross-disciplinary work by young artists in the United States and abroad.

In 1999 Hopkins assumed the presidency along with Joseph V. Melillo—she ran the business, and he oversaw the programming. As funding and programs increased and the building was refurbished, BAM served to anchor both Brooklyn's renaissance as well as the borough's eventual takeover from Manhattan as the heart of the City's cutting edge. BAM also anchored a vast cultural district, which today includes BRIC, the Mark Morris Dance Center, and the massive, 18,000-seat Barclays Center, which, since opening in 2012, has hosted the likes of P!nk, Andrea Bocelli, and Jay Z.

During her tenure, Hopkins guided an expansion to a second, and then a third, building and she set plans in motion for two more additions: BAM Strong, which will have exhibition space and a new facility to house BAM's archives along with additional cinemas and an educational studio. By the time Hopkins retired in 2015, the annual operating budget had increased from $21 to $54 million, with annual attendance exceeding 700,000. She also established an endowment of $100 million, including pledges, where previously none existed.

In 2014, Hopkins was one of only two women (with Diane von Fürstenberg) in *Crain's New York Business'* inaugural ten-member Hall of Fame. But her colleagues came up with a more personal tribute: the new building, with an anticipated completion in 2018, will be called the "BAM Karen."

THE WISECRACKERS

From the age of thirteen, when she won an amateur night competition at Keeney's Theatre in Brooklyn, **FANNY BRICE** (1891–1951) had pursued the dream of being an entertainer. That dream led her to singing in a burlesque house in 1910, where she so impressed Florenz Ziegfeld Jr.—who'd opened his wildly popular "Follies" in 1907—that he offered the singer $75 a week to star in his show, a proposal she jumped at. A natural goof with an innate sweetness, Brice quickly became a sensation, helping the Follies become *the* event of the Broadway season, talked about from coast to coast.

Brice's warmth and self-deprecating style captivated audiences and drew crowds, despite the fact that she poked fun at nearly everyone. In keeping with accepted practice of the era, she sang in blackface, performed with fake Irish and German accents, and routinely mimicked Yiddish—stunts for which Broadway's entertainment value would become legendary.

In 1916 she introduced her comic version of a dying swan ballet, which became an iconic vaudeville routine. But she had other sides to her repertoire as well: in 1921 her heart-rending rendition of the torch song "My Man" brought her international fame.

After becoming the first woman to star in a motion picture with sound, in

1938 Brice began a weekly radio program, during which she played a character of her invention, terrible toddler Baby Snooks. Despite competition from the increasingly popular new medium of television in the late 1940s, Brice remained one of the City's biggest stars up until her death in 1951. Her wit would later be memorialized by Barbra Streisand in *Funny Girl*, a 1968 film about Brice's life.

In 1974, instead of relying on reruns of *The Tonight Show Starring Johnny Carson*, NBC wanted original programming for the 11:30 PM Saturday timeslot. They turned to Dick Ebersol, who got a pitch for a comedy variety show from a Canadian-born TV writer named Lorne Michaels.

Casting *Saturday Night Live* the following year, Michaels's first hire was comedic actress **GILDA RADNER** (1946–1989), who he'd seen perform with the Second City comedy troupe in Toronto. Having observed what he once described as "a remarkable quality to her, a goodness, which came through whatever she was doing," Michaels didn't even ask her to audition.

During her five years on the show, Radner, who had wild hair, kind eyes, and an impish grin, brought to life a series of zany and unforgettable characters that helped the New York–centered show become one of the country's preeminent platforms for comedy: a nasal-voiced, prone-to-rambling broadcaster named Roseanne Roseannadanna; Candy Slice, a masochistic punk rock star; and Baba Wawa, a spoof version of Barbara Walters. Her characters were so popular that

Radner performed them in a revue, *Gilda Live,* at Broadway's Winter Garden Theatre in 1979, which was later produced as a film.

Radner's continued feistiness and humor in the face of ovarian cancer became perhaps her most enduring legacy. A year before her death in 1989, she appeared on *It's Garry Shandling's Show* and, borrowing a line from Mark Twain, joked that "Reports of my death are greatly exaggerated."

In Radner's honor, Gene Wilder, her widower, established Gilda's Club, a free counseling center for cancer patients and their families, which today continues to be based in the West Village even after expanding into a national organization.

To be an SNL cast member, you have to be funny. To be an SNL writer, you have to be funny and scintillating. Since the show has reached as many as 20.8 million viewers, to become head writer—a position held by only fourteen people over the show's first quarter century—you have to be funny, brilliant, and unfailing.

Even though she lacked a "big hunk of meat between the legs," as an adroit predecessor once declared was helpful for humor writing, **TINA FEY** (b. 1970) was so relentlessly clever that in 1999, at just twenty-nine years old, she became the first and, so far, only female head writer for the show.

And though the program had been losing its luster for some time, in 2000, when Fey stepped in front of the cameras to coanchor *Weekend Update* (with newbie Jimmy Fallon), *SNL* regained ratings and cultural clout. It also began

an epochal shift in New York's comedy landscape: Fey, who had been one of just three women among the twenty-two-member writing staff when she joined, devised a series of sketches that broke heretofore unthinkable boundaries for female comedians—establishing that women could be just as crass and irreverent as their male counterparts. (Consider, for example, Fey's ribald 2003 sketch "Colonel Angus Comes Home," set on a plantation in the Deep South called Shady Thicket, where the primary character's name functions as a double entendre.)

She made it a priority to feature female comedians like Amy Poehler, Rachel Dratch, and Kristen Wiig. In 2004 she wrote her first screenplay, *Mean Girls*, then became one of the few, if not the only, women to write, create, and star in a network sitcom, *30 Rock*, for which she picked up an armload of Emmys.

So convincing was Fey at playing Liz Lemon, her *30 Rock* writer–main character, so cerebral did she look in a bespectacled American Express ad campaign, so mannish were the arms on the cover of her 2011 autobiography, *Bossypants*, that the City's media establishment (and Hollywood's) welcomed her as a power player. In 2013, she and sidekick Amy Poehler were asked to host the Golden Globes, an honor repeated another two times.

By continuing to produce and star in movies, create a new TV series, and write hilarious sketches that chip away at what increasingly appears to be a thinly shellacked veneer of patriarchy, Fey cut inroads through the thicket of

TINA FEY

male-dominated mass media—paths on which women like Mindy Kaling, Lena Dunham, and Phoebe Robinson continue to travel.

Nowhere was this more evident than on the stunned faces of the audience during a monologue at the 2015 Golden Globes. After noting the actor George Clooney's recent marriage to Amal Alamuddin, Fey straight-facedly delivered these lines: "Amal is a human rights lawyer who worked on the Enron case, was an advisor to Kofi Annan regarding Syria, and was selected for a three-person UN commission investigating rules of war violations in the Gaza Strip. So tonight her *husband* is getting a lifetime achievement award."

Fresh after graduating from Wellesley in 1962, **NORA EPHRON** (1941–2012), the Beverly Hills–reared daughter of two playwright/screenwriters, alighted on Manhattan Island. Seeking a career in journalism, she got a job as a mail girl at *Newsweek*. But it was the astutely witty essays she wrote for *Esquire* and *New York* in the early 1970s that grabbed readers in a way that perhaps only Dorothy Parker, Manhattan's original "it girl," had ever done before: by tapping into the deepest of human needs, wants, and fears with meringue-light quips.

After writing several TV scripts, Ephron expanded into screenwriting, turning her 1983 novel about her divorce from journalist Carl Bernstein into the screenplay for *Heartburn*. But it was through a romantic comedy about two New York neurotics, *When Harry Met Sally . . .* , that she achieved a formula that would establish her as queen of the City's creative class, embedding fierce social criticism in a populist, New York–centric comedy.

In the most unforgettable scene from *When Harry Met Sally . . .*, the actress Meg Ryan loudly and dramatically fakes an orgasm during lunch at Katz's Delicatessen, decisively ending every man's belief in his own efficaciousness (and simultaneously affirming the centrality of pickles to crucial human interactions).

When a middle-aged woman at a nearby booth (played by Estelle Reiner, the real-life mother of the film's director Rob Reiner) reacts by informing the waiter, "I'll have what she's having," it was the comedic and feminist equivalent of a one-two punch—delivered fourteen years before Fey would tip her hat to Colonel Angus.

Subsequently, Ephron became a rare triple-hyphenate in male-dominated Hollywood by writing, directing, and producing *You've Got Mail* (1998) and *Julie & Julia* (2009), a feat outmatched only by the hilarity and humanity she displayed in her crackling-with-life personal essays.

After a thirty-year break from the essay-writing genre, she published two best-selling essay collections cataloging her life in the City. At the 2015 premiere of *Everything Is Copy*, a documentary about Ephron that her son, Jacob Bernstein, began making after her death in 2012, Bernstein observed why comedy plays such an important role in human life—and in the life of the City. Comedy, he said, "exists at the intersection of bravery and ruthlessness."

INDEX OF NAMES

SELECTED BIBLIOGRAPHY

Abbott, Berenice. *Berenice Abbott, Photographer: A Modern Vision*. New York: New York Public Library, 1989.

Abbott, Karen. "The House that Polly Adler Built," *Smithsonian.com*, April 12, 2012, Accessed July 2, 2016, http://www.smithsonianmag.com/history/the-house-that-polly-adler-built-65080310.

Abzug, Bella, and Mim Kelber. *Gender Gap: Bella Abzug's Guide to Political Power for American Women*. Boston: Houghton Mifflin Company, 1984.

Anbinder, Tyler. *Five Points: The Nineteenth-Century New York City Neighborhood That Invented Tap Dance, Stole Elections, and Became the World's Most Notorious Slum*. New York: The Free Press, 2001.

Antler, Joyce. *Talking Back: Images of Jewish Women in American Popular Culture*. Hanover: University Press of New England, 1998.

Arbus, Diane. *Diane Arbus: An Aperture Monograph*. New York: Aperture, 1972.

___. *Magazine World*. New York: Aperture, 1984.

Argersinger, Jo Ann E. *The Triangle Fire: A Brief History with Documents*. Bedford Cultural Editions Series. Boston: Bedford/St. Martin's, 2009.

Asbury, Herbert. *The Gangs of New York: An Informal History of the Underworld*. New York: Vintage Books, 2008.

Baim, Tracy. *Barbara Gittings: Gay Pioneer*. Chicago: Prairie Avenue Productions, 2015.

Baker, Jean H. *Margaret Sanger: A Life of Passion*. New York: Hill and Wang, 2011.

Barbour, Hugh, ed. "Quaker Crosscurrents: Three Hundred Years of Friends in the New York Yearly Meeting." New York: Syracuse University Press, 1995.

Barnet, Andrea. *All-Night Party: The Women of Bohemian Greenwich Village and Harlem, 1913–1930*. Chapel Hill: Algonquin Books of Chapel Hill, 2004.

Beilke, Jayne R. "Partners in Distress: Jewish Philanthropy and Black Education During the Progressive Era." *American Educational History Journal* 29 (2002): 26–35.

Bergreen, Laurence. *As Thousands Cheer: The Life of Irving Berlin*. New York: Viking Penguin, 1990.

Blackburn, Julie. *With Billie: A New Look at the Unforgettable Lady Day*. New York: Vintage Books, 2005.

Blackwell, Elizabeth. *Pioneer Work in Opening the Medical Profession to Women: Autobiographical Sketches*. London: Longmans, Green, and Co., 1895.

Bloom, Samuel W. *The World as Scalpel: A History of Medical Sociology*. New York: Oxford University Press, 2002.

Bly, Nellie. *Ten Days in a Madhouse*. New York: Ian L. Munro, 1887.

Bogle, Donald. *Heat Wave: The Life and Career of Ethel Waters*. New York: HarperCollins, 2011.

Boese, Thomas. *Public Education in the City of New York: Its History, Condition and Statistics. An Official Report to the Board of Education*. New York: Harper & Brothers, 1869.

Borden, Lucille Papin. *Francesca Cabrini: Without Staff or Scrip*. New York: The Macmillan Company, 1945.

Bosworth, Patricia. *Diane Arbus: A Biography*. New York: W.W. Norton & Company, 1984.

Bourgois, Philippe. *In Search of Respect: Selling Crack in El Barrio*. New York: Cambridge University Press, 1995.

Bourne Oland, William. *History of the Public School Society of the City of New York: With Portraits of the Presidents of the Society*. New York: William Wood & Co, 1870.

Boyd, Valerie. *Wrapped in Rainbows: The Life of Zora Neale Hurston*. New York: Scribner, 2003.

Brodesser-Akner, Taffy. "Iris Apfel Doesn't Do Normcore." *The New York Times Magazine*. April 12, 2015.

Bullough, Vern L. *Before Stonewall: Activists for Gay and Lesbian Rights in Historical Context*. New York: Routledge, 2008.

Bundles, A'lelia. *On Her Own Ground: The Life and Times of Madame C.J. Walker*. New York: Scribner, 2001.

Burrows, Edwin G., and Mike Wallace. *Gotham: A History of New York City to 1898*. New York: Oxford University Press, 1999.

Caro, Robert A. *The Power Broker: Robert Moses and the Fall of New York*. New York: Alfred A. Knopf, 1974.

Carpenter, Teresa. *New York Diaries: 1609 to 2009*. New York: Modern Library, 2012.

Charyn, Jerome. *Gangsters & Gold Diggers: Old New York, the Jazz Age, and the Birth of Broadway*. New York: Thunder's Mouth Press, 2003.

Chepesiuk, Ron. *Gangsters of Harlem: The Gritty Underworld of New York's Most Famous Neighborhood*. Fort Lee, NJ: Barricade Books, 2007.

Chesler, Ellen. *Woman of Valor: Margaret Sanger and the Birth Control Movement in America*. New York: Simon & Schuster, 1992.

Cinotto, Simone. *The Italian American Table: Food Family and Community in New York City*. Urbana: University of Illinois Press, 2013.

Coleman, Catherine Brawer and Kathleen Murphy Skolnik. *The Art Deco Murals of Hildreth Meière*. New York: Andrea Monfried Editions, 2014.

Conway, J. North. *Queen of Thieves: The True Story of "Marm" Mandelbaum and Her Gangs of New York*. New York: Skyhorse, 2014.

Coss, Clare, ed. *Lillian D. Wald: Progressive Activist*. New York: The Feminist Press, 1989.

Cubberley, Ellwood Patterson. *The History of Education: Educational Practice and Progress Considered as a Phase of the Development and Spread of Western Civilization*. Riverside Textbooks in Education. Cambridge: The Riverside Press/Boston: Houghton Mifflin, 1920.

Cullen-DuPont, Kathryn. *Elizabeth Cady Stanton and Women's Liberty*. Makers of America Series. New York: Facts on File, 1992.

Dain, Norman. *Clifford W. Beers, Advocate for the Insane*. Pittsburgh: University of Pittsburgh Press, 1980.

Darien, Andrew T. *Becoming New York's Finest: Race, Gender, and the Integration of the NYPD, 1935–1980.* New York: Palgrave Macmillan, 2013.

Daugherty, Tracy. *The Last Love Song: A Biography of Joan Didion.* New York: St. Martin's Press, 2015.

De Veaux, Alexis. *Warrior Poet: A Biography of Audre Lorde.* New York: W.W. Norton & Company, 2004

De Voe, Thomas F. *The Market Book: Containing a Historical Account of the Public Markets in the Cities of New York, Boston, Philadelphia, and Brooklyn, with a Brief Description of Every Article of Human Food Sold Therein . . .* (Vol. 1.) New York: Burt Franklin, 1862.

___. *The Market Assistant: Containing a Brief Description of Every Article of Human Food Sold in the Public Markets of the Cities of New York, Boston, Philadelphia, and Brooklyn.* New York: Hurd and Houghton, 1867.

Dolkart, Andrew S. *Morningside Heights: A History of Its Architecture and Development.* New York: Columbia University Press, 1998.

Downey, Kirstin. *The Woman Behind the New Deal: The Life of Frances Perkins, FDR's Secretary of Labor and His Moral Conscience.* New York: Nan A. Talese/Doubleday, 2009.

Ephron, Nora. *Heartburn.* New York: Vintage Books, 1983.

Epstein, Helen. "The Doctor Who Made a Revolution." *The New York Review of Books.* Sept 26, 2013 issue. nybooks.com/articles/2013/09/26/doctor-who-made-revolution.

Faderman, Lillian. *The Gay Revolution: The Story of the Struggle.* New York: Simon & Schuster, 2015.

Fairstein, Linda A. *Oral History Memoir at the NYPL.* June and November, 1994.

Federal Writers' Project. *The Italians of New York: A Survey Prepared by Workers of the Federal Writers' Project, Works Progress Administration in the City of New York.* New York: Random House, 1938.

Fitzpatrick, Edward Augustus. *The Educational Views and Influence of De Witt Clinton.* New York: Teachers College, Columbia University, 1911.

Felker, Clay, ed. *The Power Game: Edited by Clay Felker from the Pages of New York Magazine.* New York: Simon & Schuster, 1969.

Ferraro, Geraldine A., and Linda Bird Francke. *Ferraro: My Story.* New York: Bantam Books, 1985.

Fitzpatrick, Kevin C. *A Journey into Dorothy Parker's New York.* Berkeley: Roaring Forties Press, 2005.

Flexner, Eleanor, and Ellen Fitzpatrick. *Century of Struggle: The Women's Rights Movement in the United States.* Cambridge, MA: Belknap Press of Harvard University, 1959.

Flinn, Caryl. *Brass Diva: The Life and Legends of Ethel Merman.* Berkeley: University of California Press, 2007.

Frank, Lisa Tendrich, ed. *An Encyclopedia of American Women at War: From the Home Front to the Battlefields.* Santa Barbara: ABC-CLIO, 2013.

Frederick, Christine. *The New Housekeeping: Efficiency Studies in Home Management*. Garden City: Doubleday, Page & Company, 1913.

___. *Selling Mrs. Consumer*. New York: The Business Bourse, 1929.

Gabriel, Mary. *Notorious Victoria: The Life of Victoria Woodhull, Uncensored*. Chapel Hill: Algonquin Books of Chapel Hill, 1998.

Gallo, Marcia M. *Different Daughters: A History of the Daughters of Bilitis and the Rise of the Lesbian Rights Movement*. Emeryville: Seal Press, 2007.

Gilbert, Lynn, and Gaylen Moore. *Particular Passions: Talks with Women Who Have Shaped Our Times*. New York: Potter Style, 1981.

Goddard, Ives. The Origin and Meaning of the Name "Manhattan," vol. 91, no. 4, pp. 277–293. New York History. Fall 2010.

Grant, Joanne. *Ella Baker: Freedom Bound*. New York: John Wiley & Sons, 1998.

Greene, Gael. "Cafe Chauveron as Love Object." *New York*, Vol. 2 #34, pp. 60-61.

Greene, Gael. *Insatiable: Tales from a Life of Delicious Excess*. New York: Time Warner Book Group, 2006.

Griffith, Elisabeth. *In Her Own Right: The Life of Elizabeth Cady Stanton*. New York: Oxford University Press, 1984.

Grimes, William. *Appetite City: A Culinary History of New York*. New York: North Point Press, 2009.

Hall, Joan Wylie, ed. *Conversations with Audre Lorde*. Literary Conversations Series. Jackson: University Press of Mississippi, 2004.

Hell, Richard. *I Dreamed I Was a Very Clean Tramp: An Autobiography*. New York: Ecco, 2013.

Hemenway, Robert E. *Zora Neale Hurston: A Literary Biography*. Urbana: University of Illinois Press, 1977.

Hermes, Will. *Love Goes to Buildings on Fire: Five Years in New York That Changed Music Forever*. New York: Farrar, Straus and Giroux, 2011.

Holmes, Julia. *100 New Yorkers: A Guide to Illustrious Lives & Locations*. New York: The Little Bookroom, 2004.

hooks, bell. *Teaching to Transgress: Education As the Practice of Freedom*. New York: Routledge, 1994.

Horovitz, Bruce. "Queen of advertising tells all" in *USA Today*, May 2002, accessed July 13, 2016, http://usatoday30.usatoday.com/money/covers/2002-05-03-wells-lawrence.htm.

Howe, Irving. "The New York Intellectuals," *Commentary*, October 1968, Vol. 46, Numb. 4, pp. 29-51.

Hughes, Langston. *The Big Sea: An Autobiography*. American Century Series. New York: Alfred A. Knopf, 1940.

Hunt, Viola K. "Why an Aging English Dowager Was Labeled a Dangerous Woman," *Liberty*, September/October 1987, pp. 3-4.

Hurston, Zora Neale. *Dust Tracks on a Road: An Autobiography*. Chronology by Henry Louis Gates, Jr. New York: HarperPerennial, 1990.

Italia, Bob. *Clara Hale: Mother to Those Who Needed One (Everyone Contributes)*. Edna, MN: Abdo & Daughters, 1993.

Jackson, Kenneth T., ed. *The Encyclopedia of New York City*. New Haven: Yale University Press, 1995

Jacobs, Jane. *The Death and Life of Great American Cities*. New York: Random House, 1961.

James, Edward T., Janet Wilson James, and Paul S. Boyer, eds. *Notable American Women: A Biographical Dictionary*, 1607-1950, Volume 1: A–F. Cambridge, MA: Belknap Press of Harvard University, 1971.

Jones, Grace, and Paul Morley. *I'll Never Write My Memoirs*. New York: Gallery Books, 2015.

Keefe, Patrick Radden. "The Snakehead," *The New Yorker*, April 24, 2006.

Kert, Bernice. *Abby Aldrich Rockefeller: The Woman in the Family*. New York: Random House, 1993.

Khandelwal, Madhulika S. *Becoming American, Being Indian: An Immigrant Community in New York City*. Ithaca: Cornell University Press, 2002.

Kitaeff, Jack. *Jews in Blue: The Jewish American Experience in Law Enforcement*. Amherst: Cambria Press, 2006.

Klein, Alexander, ed. *The Empire City: A Treasury of New York*. New York: Rinehart & Company, 1955.

Lacey, Robert. *Model Woman: Eileen Ford and the Business of Beauty*. New York: HarperCollins, 2015.

Lange, Alexandra. "Dreams Built and Broken: On Ada Louise Huxtable." *The Nation*, April 15, 2013.

Lawrence, Mary Wells. *A Big Life in Advertising*. New York: Alfred A. Knopf, 2002.

Levine, Suzanne Braun, and Mary Thom. *Bella Abzug: How One Tough Broad from the Bronx Fought Jim Crow and Joe McCarthy, Pissed Off Jimmy Carter, Battled for the Rights of Women and Workers, Rallied Against War and For the Planet, and Shook Up Politics Along the Way*. New York: Farrar, Straus and Giroux, 2007.

Lorde, Audre. *From a Land Where Other People Live*. Chicago: Broadside Press, 1973.

___. *Sister Outsider: Essays & Speeches*. The Crossing Press Feminist Series. New York: Ten Speed Press, 1984.

___. *New York Head Shop and Museum*. Detroit: Broadside Press, 1975.

Lutz, Alma. *Susan B. Anthony: Rebel, Crusader, Humanitarian*. Boston: Beacon Press, 1959.

Lynskey, Dorian. 33 *Revolutions Per Minute: A History of Protest Songs*. London: Faber and Faber, 2010.

Lyons, Sophie. *Queen of the Underworld*. New York: Combustion Books, 2013, anniversary edition.

Macpherson, Myra. *The Scarlet Sisters: Sex, Scandal, and Suffrage in the Gilded Age*. New York: Twelve, 2014.

Mahler, Jonathan. *Ladies and Gentlemen, the Bronx Is Burning: 1977, Baseball, Politics, and the Battle for the Soul of a City*. New York: Picador, 2005.

Margolick, David. *Strange Fruit: The Biography of a Song*. New York: HarperCollins, 2001.

Maynard, Theodore. *Too Small a World: The Life of Francesca Cabrini*. Milwaukee: The Bruce Publishing Company, 1945.

Mays, Dorothy A. *Women in Early America: Struggle, Survival, and Freedom in a New World*. Santa Barbara: ABC-CLIO, 2004.

McCarthy, Andy. "Class Act: Researching New York City Schools with Local History Collections". Online blog post dated October 20, 2014. Accessed June 19, 2016. nypl.org/blog/2014/10/20/researching-nyc-schools

Meltzer, Brad. *Heroes For My Son*. New York: HarperCollins, 2010.

Moraga, Cherríe L., and Gloria E. Anzaldúa. *This Bridge Called My Back: Writings by Radical Women of Color*. Latham, NY: Kitchen Table/Women of Color Press, 1981.

Morley, Sheridan. "A girl I met in Hawaii…," *The Times*, September 21, 1978, p. 9.

Naylor, Gloria. *The Women of Brewster Place*. New York: Viking Penguin, 1982.

Nicholson, Stuart. *Billie Holiday*. London: Victor Gollancz, 1995.

Nunez, Sigrid. *Sempre Susan: A Memoir of Susan Sontag*. New York: Atlas & Co., 2011.

O'Han , Nicholas. "Tough Economic Times Created the Rationale for One School." Online article, originally published Summer 2009. Accessed June 18, 2016. nais.org/Magazines-Newsletters/ISMagazine/Pages/The-Little-School-That-Could.aspx.

O'Neal, Hank. *Berenice Abbott: American Photographer*. New York: McGraw-Hill, 1982.

Ono, Yoko. *Grapefruit: A Book of Instructions and Drawings*. New York: Simon & Schuster, 1964.

Palmer, Archie Emerson. "The New York public school; being a history of free education in the city of New York." New York: The Macmillan Company, 1905.

Pantoja, Antonia. *Memoir of a Visionary: Antonia Pantoja*. Houston, TX: Arte Público Press 2015.

Petrash, Antonia. *More Than Petticoats: Remarkable New York Women*. Guilford, CT: TwoDot/Globe Pequot Press, 2002.

Pogrebin, Letty Cottin. *Deborah, Golda and Me: Being Female and Jewish in America*. New York: Doubleday, 1991.

Pratt, Caroline. "I Learn from Children: An Adventure in Progressive Education." New York: First Grove Press, 2014. (Originally published by Simon & Schuster in 1948).

Public School Society of New-York. *On the Establishment of Public Schools in the City of New-York*. New York: Free-School Society of New-York, 1825.

Ravitch, Diane. *The Great School Wars, New York City, 1805–1973: A History of the Public Schools as Battlefields for Change*. New York: Basic Books, 1974.

Reed, Miriam. *Margaret Sanger: Her Life in Her Words*. Fort Lee, NJ: Barricade Books, 2003.

Richman Proskauer, Bertha, and Addie Richman Altman. *Julia Richman: Two Biographical Appreciations of the Great Educator*. New York: Julia Richman High School Association, 1916.

Ridinger, Robert B., ed. *Speaking for Our Lives: Historic Speeches and Rhetoric for Gay and Lesbian Rights (1892–2000)*. Binghampton: Harrington Park Press, 2004.

Rieder, Jonathan. *Canarsie: The Jews and Italians of Brooklyn Against Liberalism*. Cambridge: Harvard University Press, 1985.

Robinson, Solon. *Hot Corn: Life Scenes in New York Illustrated.* New York: De Witt and Davenport, Publishers, 1854.

Rollyson, Carl Edmund, and Lisa Olson Paddock. *Susan Sontag: The Making of an Icon.* New York. W.W. Norton & Company, 2000.

Rutherford, Janice Williams. *Selling Mrs. Consumer: Christine Frederick and the Rise of Household Efficiency.* Athens: University of Georgia Press, 2003.

Sanger, Margaret. *What Every Girl Should Know.* New York: New York Call, 1912.

Sante, Luc. *Low Life: Lures and Snares of Old New York.* New York: Farrar, Straus and Giroux, 1991.

Sardi, Sr., Vincent and Richard Gehman. *Sardi's: The Story of a Famous Restaurant.* New York: Henry Holt and Company, 1953.

Scarborough, Kathryn E., and Pamela A. Collins. *Women in Public and Private Law Enforcement.* Boston: Butterworth-Heinemann, 2002.

Schor, Esther. *Emma Lazarus.* New York: Schocken Books, 2006.

Schreiber, Daniel. *Susan Sontag: A Biography.* Translated by David Dollenmayer. Evanston, IL: Northwestern University Press, 2014.

Schultz, William Todd. *An Emergency in Slow Motion: The Inner Life of Diane Arbus.* New York: Bloomsbury USA, 2011.

Schwartz, Arthur. *Arthur Schwartz's New York City Food: An Opinionated History and More Than 100 Legendary Recipes.* New York: Stewart, Tabori and Chang, 2004.

Sheiner, Marcy. "Maybe I could Be—Like Barbra—GAWJUS!" *Lilith* 21, (spring 1996): 10-12. Italics in original.

Sheraton, Mimi. *Eating My Words: An Appetite for Life.* New York: HarperCollins, 2004

Sherr, Lynn. *Failure Is Impossible: Susan B. Anthony in Her Own Words.* New York: Times Books, 1995.

Siebert, Muriel, with Aimee Lee Ball. *Changing the Rules: Adventures of a Wall Street Maverick.* New York: The Free Press, 2002.

Siegel, Beatrice. *Lillian Wald of Henry Street.* New York: Macmillan, 1983.

Sills, Beverly, and Lawrence Linderman. *Beverly: An Autobiography.* New York: Bantam Books, 1987.

Sivulka, Juliann. *Ad Women: How They Impact What We Need, Want, and Buy.* Amherst, NY: Prometheus Books, 2009.

Smith, Abbe, "The Bounds of Zeal in Criminal Defense: Some Thoughts on Lynne Stewart" (2002). *Georgetown Law Faculty Publications and Other Works.*

Smith, Liz. *Natural Blond.* New York: Hyperion, 2000.

Smith, Patti. *Just Kids.* New York: Ecco, 2010.

___. *M Train.* New York: Alfred A. Knopf, 2015.

Sokol, Jason. *All Eyes Are Upon Us: Race and Politics From Boston to Brooklyn: The Conflicted Soul of the Northeast.* New York: Basic Books, 2014.

Sontag, Susan. *Against Interpretation and Other Essays.* Dell Publishing Company, 1966.

___. *On Photography*. New York: Farrar, Straus and Giroux, 1977.

Spann, Edward K. *The New Metropolis: New York City, 1840–1857*. New York, Columbia University Press, 1981.

Sparkes, Boyden, and Samuel Taylor Moore. *The Witch of Wall Street: Hetty Green*. Garden City: Doubleday, Doran & Company, 1935.

Stanton, Elizabeth Cady. "Seneca Falls Keynote Address." Address presented at the Seneca Falls Convention for Civil/Political Rights of Women, Seneca Falls, NY, July 19, 1848.

Stein, Marc. *City of Sisterly and Brotherly Loves: Lesbian and Gay Philadelphia, 1945–1972*. Philadelphia: Temple University Press, 2004.

Stewart, Shirley. *The World of Stephanie St. Clair: An Entrepreneur, Race Woman and Outlaw in Early Twentieth Century Harlem*. New York: Peter Lang Publishing, 2014.

Stuart, Amanda Mackenzie. *Empress of Fashion: A Life of Diana Vreeland*. New York: Harper Collins, 2012.

Sulzberger, Iphigene Ochs, and Susan W. Dryfoos. *Iphigene: Memoirs of Iphigene Ochs Sulzberger of the New York Times Family, as Told to Her Granddaughter, Susan W. Dryfoos*. New York: Dodd, Mead, 1981.

Sung, Betty Lee. *Defiant Second Daughter: My First 90 Years*. Charleston: Advantage Media Group, 2015.

Syme, Rachel. "Learning From Elaine." *The New Yorker.com*. July 23, 2014.

Szwed, John. *Billie Holiday: The Musician and the Myth*. New York: Viking Penguin, 2015.

"Talk of the Town: Jane Grant, The New Yorker, and the Oregon Legacy of a Twentieth-Century Feminist," University of Oregon Libraries, Special Collections and University Archives, last modified September 25, 2013, accessed June 8, 2015. http://library.uoregon.edu/ec/exhibits/janegrant/exhib.html.

Tharp, Twyla. *The Creative Habit: Learn It and Use It for Life*. New York: Simon & Schuster, 2003.

Thomas, Marlo. "*The Givers*: What Made Bette Midler Go Green? A Divine Interview!" in TheHuffingtonPost.com, posted May 3, 2012.

Thompson, Dave. *Dancing Barefoot: The Patti Smith Story*. Chicago: Chicago Review Press, 2011.

Thurber, James. *The Years with Ross*. New York: Little, Brown and Company, 1957.

Underhill, Lois Beachy. *The Woman Who Ran for President: The Many Lives of Victoria Woodhull*. Bridgehampton: Bridge Works, 1995.

Vare, Ethlie Ann. *Diva: Barbara Streisand and the Making of a Superstar*. Brooklyn: Boulevard Books, 1996.

Vespa, Mary. "Fran Lebowitz Is New York's Answer to Erma Bombeck: the Bette Midler of Belles Lettres." People, September 4, 1978.

Wald, Lillian D. *Windows on Henry Street*. Boston: Little, Brown and Company, 1939.

Ward, Geoffrey C., and Ken Burns. *Not For Ourselves Alone: The Story of Elizabeth Cady Stanton and Susan B. Anthony*. New York: Alfred A. Knopf, 2001.

Ward, Harry M. *The War For Independence and the Transformation of American Society*. New York: Routledge, 1999.

Wendell, Eric. *Patti Smith: America's Punk Rock Rhapsodist*. Lanham, MD: Rowman & Littlefield, 2015.

Winslow, Barbara. *Shirley Chisholm: Catalyst for Change*. Lives of American Women Series. Boulder: Westview Press, 2014.

Wintz, Cary D., and Paul Finkelman. "Encyclopedia of the Harlem Renaissance." Volume 1 A-J. New York: Routledge, 2004.

Woll, Allen. *Black Musical Theatre: From Coontown to Dreamgirls*. Baton Rouge: Louisiana State University Press, 1989.

Wood, William H.S. *Friends of the City of New York in the Nineteenth Century*. New York: Privately Printed, 1904.

Woolley, Edward Mott. "Tom Rowland: Peanuts." *McClure's Magazine* 42, no. 2 (November 1913–April 1914), 183–189.

ACKNOWLEDGMENTS

A wide array of scholars, journalists, researchers, friends, family members and even strangers suggested women to be considered for this volume. Their ideas were inspiring and, in many cases, incorporated into the book. All errors of fact or judgment are mine alone.

I am especially grateful to those who provided interviews about their areas of expertise or helped in tracking down the right sources, including Tyler Anbinder, Michael Arena, Charlie Bagli, Simeon Bankoff, Chris Bartlett, Peter Blauner, Beth Broome, Lucille Burrascano, Laurie Fendrich, Andrew Friedman, Sr. Catherine Garry, Todd Gitlin, David Gonzalez, Penelope Green, William Grimes, Daniel Hertzberg, Tonya Hopkins, Charles Kaiser, Dorothy Kallins, Jerome Kohn, Ronald A. Kurtz, Beth Lebowitz, John Leland, Barry Lewis, Dr. Elizabeth Lorde-Rollins, Elaine Louie, Geoffrey Mark, Sylvia Martinez, Laurence Maslon, Cathleen McGuigan, Randolph Michael McLaughlin, Paul Moakley, Julia Moskin, Hank O'Neal, Matthew Payne, Peter Plagens, Robin Pogrebin, Barbara Raab, Diane Ravitch, David Rieff, Ozzie Rodriguez, Jody Rosen, Fran Morris Rosman, Dan Saltzstein, Izzy Sanabria, Arthur Schwartz, Kim Severson, Todd Simmons, Arthur Sulzberger, Jr., Kay Tobin Lahusen, Mike Wallace, Jamie Wellford, Jan Whitaker, Jonathan Zimmerman, Curtis Zunigha, and Tracy Zwick.

Several friends and loved ones, including Jerry Adler, Joni Dwyer, Stefania Geraci, Barbara Kantrowitz, Mariah LeBlanc, Linda Ryan, Sima Saran, Andrea Sluchan, Peg Tyre, and Leslee Vichengrad, provided immeasurable kindness and support.

Peter J. Scelto, a lifelong New York-ophile, provided inspiration, and C. Michele Simon generously helped with several weeks of childcare.

I would especially like to thank Louise Mirrer, President of the New-York Historical Society, who assured me that no single book or exhibit could ever tell the whole story, and former NYHS president Kenneth T. Jackson, who first exposed me to the City's many stirring histories in his Columbia University classroom twenty years ago. I am also thankful for the reference librarians (and Maureen Maryanski in particular) at the NYHS library, the Brooklyn Public Library, and the New York Public Library, which remain among the City's most important institutions.

The book would not have been possible without Susan Szeliga and Anna Bernstein, intrepid researchers who tracked down endless books and documents and frequently shared their own astute observations. Thank you.

Cindy Rosenthal, a lifelong New Yorker, generously collected and organized the names of more than two hundred other influential women.

After an exhausting search trying to prove the negative existence of Hell-Cat Maggie, Luc Sante generously acknowledged that in the years since publishing *Low Life: Lures and Snares of Old New York*, he has come to believe that she (and other characters) did not exist as described by Herbert Asbury in 1928.

I am deeply indebted to Laura Mazer, one of the finest editors of her generation, not only for envisioning this book and entrusting me to write it, but for taking the time many years ago to share words of wisdom with a green reporter who really needed them.

And to my husband, who, many years ago in a Park Slope kitchen, looked directly into my eyes and lovingly told me what I most needed to hear.

ABOUT THE AUTHOR

JULIE SCELFO is a frequent contributor to *The New York Times*, where her stories about how we live routinely appear on the *Times*'s most e-mailed list. Prior to joining the *Times* in 2007, Scelfo was a Correspondent at *Newsweek*, where she covered breaking news and wrote about society and human behavior. She covered the events of September 11, 2001, live from lower Manhattan, then reported extensively on the attack's environmental and emotional aftermath.

Scelfo lives with her family in New York City, where she rides a push-scooter to ease travel back and forth between neighborhoods. She is a member of PEN America, a supporter of Narrative 4, and believes radical empathy is where it's at. More information about her work can be found at www.juliescelfo.com.

Photo by Johannes Kroemer

ABOUT THE ILLUSTRATOR

HALLIE HEALD is an illustrator and stylist living and working in New York City. Her work has appeared in various magazines, including *Darling, Galore, Vogue India, Jute, Tantalum,* and *MODO* magazines. Her styling clients have included Theory, Bloomingdales, Macy's, Victoria's Secret, Helmut Lang, and DKNY. For more about Hallie Heald and her work, please visit hehdesignsny.com.